KV-577-791

CONTENTS

Part Four: Perfecting Your Work

business english

by Annie Noble

Chambers

CHAMBERS
An imprint of Chambers Harrap Publishers Ltd
7 Hopetoun Crescent
Edinburgh EH7 4AY

First published by Chambers Harrap Publishers Ltd 2007
© Chambers Harrap Publishers Ltd 2007

A CIP catalogue record for this book is available from the British Library.

ISBN 978 0550 10325 3

Editor: Ian Brookes
Prepress Controller: Becky Pickard

Designed and typeset by Chambers Harrap Publishers Ltd, Edinburgh
Printed and bound in Spain by GraphyCems

Introduction

Everyone studies English at school, but when people try to put this learning into practice in the workplace, it often seems that they are not properly equipped to communicate effectively. Both knowledge and practical ability are missing, and this can not only damage the organization you work for but also hamper your career path.

This book is designed to address those gaps and weaknesses. It aims to equip you with the tools and skills you need to be able to write all the different types of documents you are likely to produce during your working life – and to write them clearly and effectively. It is packed with examples so you can see words in action. There are lots of exercises, so you can test your knowledge as you go. But, perhaps most important of all, it aims to give you confidence in your writing and in your knowledge of the written word, so you can not only produce documents of a far higher quality but can also contribute to other people's work.

Why is English important in business?

Any organization needs to communicate to a variety of audiences: to its staff, its customers, its suppliers, its shareholders and any other stakeholder group. And writing remains the primary method of communication: perhaps even more so today, with e-mail supplanting the telephone for much internal and external communication. If you get that communication wrong, relationships may be damaged, orders may be lost, investment may be refused, staff may become demotivated, and suppliers may be alienated.

What you write doesn't go away. Unlike a conversation, it can be revisited time and again. So any mistakes are magnified and any lack of understanding soon becomes common knowledge. But get it right and it can make a positive impression.

INTRODUCTION

How to use this book

Business English is broken down into four separate but complementary units.

Part One is all about the language you use and the way you write. It is split into five sections:

* **Sentences and paragraphs**: how these basic building blocks of writing work; how to make them clear and effective.

* **Effective writing style**: choosing the best word; cutting out unnecessary words; making sure your writing says what you mean it to say.

* **Common misunderstandings about grammar**: debunking a few myths about what you can and can't write.

* **Good punctuation**: from apostrophes to commas to quotation marks, and all points in between.

* **Confusing words**: avoiding some common vocabulary mistakes which would lessen the impact of your work.

Throughout Part One there are exercises to test your knowledge as you go along.

Part Two focuses on the key documents you will produce during your working life. These comprise:

* **Letters, e-mails, faxes and memos**: helping you to improve structure, tone and impact of the most fundamental written communications.

* **Materials for meetings**: how to prepare agendas which lead to successful meetings; and how to write minutes and contact reports which accurately reflect and clearly summarize proceedings.

* **Reports, proposals and plans**: how to plan, structure and write these extended pieces of work.

* **Electronic presentations**: how to prepare presentations which will support rather than distract when using software such as Microsoft Office PowerPoint®.

Part Three looks at other communications which your organization may create. They may not be your specific responsibility, but if you understand them, you are better placed to contribute and comment on them. This section looks at how they are produced and the questions you should ask when reviewing them. It covers:

- **Press releases**: the mysterious world of communicating with the public via the press.
- **Leaflets and brochures**: planning content; getting the tone right; using persuasive words.
- **Direct mail**: taking letters a stage further to create powerful selling tools.
- **Newsletters**: identifying the right tone and the best content.
- **Websites**: every organization has one, but how can you make it really work for you?
- **Financial communications**: a word of warning.

Part Four takes your writing skills a stage further, to help you plan, structure, review and revise. Taking time over your work will make it more powerful and more successful. This section looks at:

- **Planning**: how to get over those first hurdles before you even put finger to keyboard.
- **Drafting**: getting started and then filling in the substance around your plan.
- **Reviewing and revising**: changing and improving your work.
- **Shortening**: how do you cut it back if it's too long for the purpose?
- **Summarizing**: the steps you need to take to produce a summary which might make all the difference as to whether the reader looks at the rest of a document.
- **Proofreading and house style**: helping you to achieve accuracy and consistency not only in your own documents but also across your entire organization.

By the end, you will be better equipped to produce clear, concise and effective business English.

Glossary of grammatical terms

adjective a word used to describe a noun: a *warm* day; a *happy* man

adverb a word used to describe a verb: he ran *fast*; the products sold *well*

clause a unit of words which may or may not stand alone as a sentence

conjunction a linking word, such as *and, but, whether, although*

noun a naming word, such as *man, woman, company, proposal, office*

paragraph a group of sentences that stand together

phrase any unit of words, not necessarily capable of standing alone as a sentence

preposition a word that links with a noun, such as *up, with, down, by*

pronoun something that replaces a noun but refers to it: *it, he, she, they*

sentence the largest unit to which the rules of grammar apply; this is a group of words which is complete and needs nothing else to make it complete

verb a word that expresses an action, mental process or state of being, such as *run, walk, sell, buy, think, stand*

Part One

The Basics

THE BASICS

Before you can expect to produce good and clear English in letters, reports or e-mails, you need to get the basics right. So the place to start is with the building blocks of writing: sentences and paragraphs. Once you understand what they are, how they work and how best to structure them, you can then move on to producing documents which communicate effectively.

This opening section will start by explaining how to construct correct sentences and paragraphs so that your documents are clear and easy to read.

It will then look at the words you use: how to choose the most effective words and phrases and how to be economical with the number of words you use. It will also debunk some grammatical myths, before looking at that fundamental part of sentences and paragraphs: good punctuation.

Finally, there is an exploration of some vocabulary which is often misused: confusing words and words used in error. Making these mistakes can undermine your writing, so it's vital to avoid them. By increasing your understanding and knowledge of what is right and wrong in the English language, your confidence will grow and this will be reflected in the style and tone of your writing.

You'll find plenty of exercises to test your knowledge throughout this section. At the very end, there is a quiz which will bring together many of the areas covered. It will help you assess how much you have absorbed.

Sentences and paragraphs

What is a sentence?

Firstly, what is a sentence? A definition that might be familiar to you is that it is something 'which starts with a capital letter and ends with a full stop'. However, this can be misleading; the following phrases follow these criteria but they are not sentences:

> *No parking.*
>
> *Traditional food purveyor.*
>
> *Gentlemen's outfitters.*

A sentence is something more: it is a grammatical construction which can stand alone without feeling incomplete. It is built according to the agreed rules of grammar, and it is the largest unit to which the rules of grammar apply. (We'll see later that a paragraph is merely a collection of sentences rather than a grammatical construction.)

The shortest sentence has a subject and a finite verb (a verb that describes a complete action):

> *Peter cried.*

Peter is the subject; *cried* is the verb.

Most simple sentences have a subject, a verb and an object:

> *John trimmed the hedge.*

John is the subject; *trimmed* is the verb; *the hedge* is the object.

SENTENCES AND PARAGRAPHS

A sentence is not to be confused with a fragment, which needs something else to complete it, as in this example:

> *Rising and falling as they went.*

This needs something more to make it a full sentence:

> *Rising and falling as they went, the horses slowly swam across the river.*

The sentence now has two parts: a 'main clause' and a 'secondary clause'. The main clause can stand by itself as a complete sentence; the secondary clause cannot.

✔ *The horses slowly swam across the river.*

✗ *Rising and falling as they went.*

Another way of looking at this is to think of the two separate clauses as a control unit and a support unit. Look at this clause:

> *The shop sells furniture*

This is a control unit and a complete sentence.

Now consider this clause:

> *Especially hand-crafted chairs*

This is a support unit and not a complete sentence.

But see what happens when we put the two together:

> *The shop sells furniture, especially hand-crafted chairs.*

Now we have a control unit plus a support unit and so the support unit can stand as part of a complete sentence.

Support units can be used at different places in a sentence, either before, after, or in the middle of a control unit.

Placing a support unit first sets the scene for the sentence, as in these examples:

> To tell you the truth, I couldn't care less.
>
> His argument in tatters, Peter walked out of the room.
>
> With so many leads, the client was delighted.

By splitting open the control unit and placing the support unit in the middle, you can give more information to the reader. You should generally put this type of support unit between two commas, brackets or dashes:

> The new admin assistant – a very efficient woman – soon found herself in demand.
>
> The old mansion, our company's HQ since 1958, was on fire.
>
> The car park (which can take 150 cars) is in danger of flooding.

Placing the support unit at the end of the control unit gives it more impact and a stronger feeling of adding extra information:

> Telnet's workers get free lunches, sometimes twice a week.
>
> Jon went home, although he didn't want to.

Practice exercise

Identify the complete sentences (control units) and the fragments (support units). Check your answers on page 183.

1 The staff took their holidays.
2 At the quietest time of the year.
3 Holding on to the desk for support.
4 Peter stood to make the presentation.
5 The office will open at 10am.
6 To allow for cleaning.

SENTENCES AND PARAGRAPHS

Sentence length

Short, concise sentences communicate your point more clearly than sentences which ramble on and on. As a guide, sentences should be no more than 15 to 20 words long. However, while short sentences have a sense of vigour and urgency and keep your readers on their toes, a succession of short sentences soon becomes repetitive and boring. So variety is the answer: keep most sentences short, but also include the occasional longer sentence to add variety and improve the flow.

Keeping sentences short

There are several techniques you can use to make a long, flabby sentence shorter and more punchy. It may be that you can split it into separate sentences. Look at this example:

> *The technology is called the Advanced Dispensing System (ADS) and provides high levels of security for dispensing drugs, while also enabling clinicians to remotely monitor and, if required, remotely control drug usage in real time.*

This sentence contains 35 words. The meaning would be far clearer if it were split into two, by simply making the first clause into a separate sentence and adding a subject for the verb at the beginning of the new second sentence to make it stand by itself:

> *The technology is called the Advanced Dispensing System (ADS). It provides high levels of security for dispensing drugs, while also enabling clinicians to remotely monitor and, if required, remotely control drug usage in real time.*

Now look at this example:

> *Resources such as the online InfoBank (only available to supported customers), containing almost 500 technical articles on all aspects of using our software, further assist in our goal of providing all developers with a superior level of support.*

This sentence runs to 38 words and is very difficult to follow: it is full of separate clauses which don't quite fit together smoothly. It can be improved by splitting it into two and changing the order of the information to make it more logical:

> *Resources such as the online InfoBank further assist in our goal of providing all developers with a superior level of support. InfoBank, which is only available to supported customers, contains almost 500 technical articles on all aspects of using our software.*

Another way of keeping sentences short and snappy is to cut out unnecessary words. Look at this example:

> *An example of financial advisory services at Jumbo Bank is the provision of these services to low-income households.*

The sentence could be rewritten using 11 words rather than 18:

> *For example, Jumbo Bank provides financial advisory services to low-income households.*

Note the changes that have been made to shorten the sentence:

- *An example of* has become *For example*.
- The subject of the sentence has changed from *An example* to *Jumbo Bank*.
- *The provision of* has become *provides*.
- The repetition of *services* has been removed.

The last paragraph demonstrates a further technique for avoiding excessively long sentences: using bullet points. Sometimes sentences become too long because they comprise what is in effect a list. If so, you can make your meaning much clearer through using bullets.

SENTENCES AND PARAGRAPHS

Consider this example:

> *The range has many benefits, which include corrosion-resistant components and panels, scratch-resistant surfaces, concealed fixings, double-fixed locks to prevent removal, overhead modesty screens to deter peeping Toms and rounded internal corners to aid cleaning.*

By splitting this down into bullets, these benefits become much clearer:

> *The range has many benefits, which include:*
> - *corrosion-resistant components and panels*
> - *scratch-resistant surfaces*
> - *concealed fixings*
> - *double-fixed locks to prevent removal*
> - *overhead modesty screens to deter peeping Toms*
> - *rounded internal corners to aid cleaning*

Practice exercise

1 Break the following long sentence into shorter sentences. Check your answers on page 183.

> *We seek to grow our business by offering innovative leathers which are differentiated from competing products by their performance, quality and consistency and which are backed by the highest standards of customer service.*

2 Break the following long sentence into shorter sentences:

> *Smith's share price is down, sales are under pressure, it has withdrawn some of its promotional activities and the Health Protection Agency has linked the company to an outbreak of a rare strain of salmonella among 45 people by describing it as 'an exact match of that [strain] found in the product'.*

Joining sentences together

While clear English is often achieved through using short sentences, excessive use of short sentences can make your writing seem unsophisticated and weak. It is sometimes better to join two short sentences together to make one, more sophisticated, unit.

Look at the following simple sentences:

> *The cat sat on the desk.*
>
> *The dog ran down the road.*
>
> *The lorry drove away.*
>
> *The delegates laughed at their mistakes.*
>
> *The trainer wasn't happy.*
>
> *The observer felt uncomfortable.*

You can join simple sentences together using words such as *and*, *but*, *whereas* and *although*. (These 'joining words' are called conjunctions.)

In these examples, simple sentences have been joined together using conjunctions to make longer ones:

> *The cat sat on the desk and the dog ran down the road.*
>
> *The delegates laughed at their mistakes but the trainer wasn't happy.*
>
> *The delegates laughed at their mistakes although the observer felt uncomfortable.*

A key point to remember is that it is not enough to use just a comma to join complete sentences together:

✗ *The cat sat on the desk, the dog ran down the road.*

✗ *The delegates laughed at their mistakes, the trainer wasn't happy.*

SENTENCES AND PARAGRAPHS

If you join three sentences together, you can use a comma to make the first link, but you need at least one conjunction:

> *The cat sat on the desk, the dog ran down the road but the lorry drove away.*

> *The delegates laughed at their mistakes, although the trainer wasn't happy and the observer felt uncomfortable.*

Once again, using just commas is not enough:

✗ *The cat sat on the desk, the dog ran down the road, the lorry drove away.*

✗ *The delegates laughed at their mistakes, the trainer wasn't happy, the observer felt uncomfortable.*

Practice exercise

Join these sentences together to make a more sophisticated sentence. Check your answers on page 183.

1 *It was a bright evening. The birds chirped in the trees.*
2 *It was a bright evening. The birds chirped in the trees. Annie sat in the garden.*
3 *It was a bright evening. The house was dark when they arrived. They turned on the lights.*
4 *We need to develop a new programme which will attract new customers. We need to assure existing clients that this will not affect them.*
5 *We need to develop a new programme which will attract new customers. We need to assure existing clients that this will not affect them. We need to prove this to them.*

Active and passive sentences

In an active sentence the subject carries out the action described by the verb. An active sentence usually follows the pattern of subject + verb + object:

> *Peter opened his diary.*

In this example *Peter* is the subject; *opened* is the verb; *his diary* is the object.

In a passive sentence the subject has something done to it. A passive sentence usually follows the pattern of subject + passive verb + agent:

> *The diary was opened by Peter.*

In this example *the diary* is the subject; *was opened* is the verb; *Peter* is the agent.

Active sentences are far more punchy and tend to be shorter. It is good practice to use active sentences rather than passive. It will make your writing clearer and more succinct.

However, there are some occasions when using the passive can help to communicate what you are trying to say more effectively. The passive can be used as a more tactful way of writing, taking the full impact away from something you do not want to stress or draw attention to:

> *Journal entry errors were made in the books.*

By using the active (*Our accountant made journal entry errors in the books*), all the blame goes on a named person – but perhaps this is not what you want to stress. By using the passive, the person remains anonymous and the focus of the sentence is on simply admitting there were errors.

The passive can be used to deal with tricky matters, such as being courteous when asking staff to do something. An active sentence structure here might come across as authoritarian:

> *You have not completed your timesheets.*

Turning it around into the passive takes some of the sting out of the reminder or rebuke:

> *Timesheets have not been completed.*

SENTENCES AND PARAGRAPHS

The passive can also be used to stress an important part of the sentence. In this example, the active sentence structure puts the emphasis on the organization offering the loan:

> *We will offer a secured loan to the customer.*

Depending on the context, it may be important to emphasize that it is a secured (rather than an unsecured) loan which will be offered. Making the sentence passive will bring the important words to the front:

> *A secured loan will be offered to the customer.*

The passive is used frequently in business communications such as reports, as it enables personal references to be eliminated and so makes the document sound more independent:

> ✗ *I carried out interviews with 50 shoppers and 30 owners.*

> ✔ *Interviews were carried out with 50 shoppers and 30 owners.*

> ✗ *I therefore recommend that the office should be relocated to Swindon.*

> ✔ *It is recommended that the office should be relocated to Swindon.*

Practice exercise

Turn these passive sentences into active sentences. Check your answers on page 184.

1 *A more concise presentation of ideas needs to be organized.*
2 *The evidence has been carefully considered and there seem to be grounds for disciplinary action. The managing director has been informed by letter and his reply is expected on Thursday.*
3 *During the programme, outbound calls will be made to customers to assess their willingness to purchase.*
4 *Data will be collected and presented each month.*

Paragraphs

A paragraph is simply a logical collection of sentences. Unlike sentences, paragraphs are not governed by rules of grammar: they are simply there as a visual aid to lead the reader through the text by splitting it into manageable chunks.

In some written communications – in particular essays and other academic materials – paragraphs tend to be as long as is needed to argue a particular point. In business English, however, it is best to keep paragraphs short and snappy.

When deciding how long a paragraph should be, consider your likely readers and their attention span. There is nothing more offputting than having long wedges of text without any breaks. So keep in mind the following guidelines:

- Aim for a minimum of two and a maximum of four sentences in a paragraph.
- Avoid one-sentence paragraphs, as they feel disjointed and weak. If a one-sentence paragraph comprises one long sentence, you may need to split that sentence into two or more sentences to make a more effective paragraph.
- Look at sentences for their sense: is there a logical break where a paragraph might end and a new one start?
- Is the paragraph so long that it will put the readers off? If so, can it be split up and a linking word or an introductory phrase added to restart the flow after the break?

Look at this example:

> *Looking to the future, work moves on apace with the plans for rebuilding the school. There is a very tight work schedule, to meet a deadline to submit full curriculum and rooming analyses to the Department for Education and Skills by 31 March, and at the same time the architects must submit working drawings. At this stage, the Government will give firm approval*

to proceed and we shall then be setting up a range of working and consultation groups to define the vision for the new school. We already have student groups forming to shadow the design team, including project management, design and alternative energy, and will be seeking to draw support from a range of stakeholders, including parents, governors and the wider community to help us in this important work. Two things are certain: firstly, that in three years' time the tired buildings in which we now work will be about to pass into history, and secondly, our commitment to ensuring we keep focused on the needs of our current students in the intervening period remains absolute.

You will probably agree that this paragraph is intimidatingly long. It needs to be split. This can be achieved by a combination of inserting paragraph breaks and some linking words, and turning a long sentence into three separate sentences:

Looking to the future, work moves on apace with the plans for rebuilding the school. There is a very tight work schedule, to meet a deadline to submit full curriculum and rooming analyses to the Department for Education and Skills by 31 March, and at the same time the architects must submit working drawings.

Following this, the Government will give firm approval to proceed and we shall then be setting up a range of working and consultation groups to define the vision for the new school. We already have student groups forming to shadow the design team, including project management, design and alternative energy, and will be seeking to draw support from a range of stakeholders, including parents, governors and the wider community, to help us in this important work.

Two things are certain. Firstly, in three years' time the tired buildings in which we now work will be about

> *to pass into history. Secondly, our commitment to ensuring we keep focused on the needs of our current students in the intervening period remains absolute.*

Now that it has been split into manageable chunks, the text is much easier to read.

Practice exercise

Break the following long paragraph into shorter paragraphs. Check your answer on page 184.

> *For a consulting company dedicated to improving healthcare through quality and business analysis, it was critical to find a flexible, reliable and low-cost solution that could grow with their needs. As a result of the Instorage architecture, which uses standard Ethernet switching for host and storage array connectivity, DHS achieves much better performance than its previous DAS environment. The scalable Instorage solution enables DHS to expand the IP SAN using in-house resources. As a result, researchers have faster and more reliable access to data, enabling them to process and analyze patient records and test results more effectively. In addition, the company can start more research projects without concerns about storage capacity.*

Effective paragraph structure

Now that we have established what a paragraph is, let's look at some ways of making paragraphs work effectively. One simple way of making a paragraph work is to make the main point first and then support it with argument or fact. Look at this example:

> *Our range of partitions offers clear advantages over other, similar systems. It is particularly suited to swimming-pool changing rooms. Every element is water-resistant and will not degrade in a wet environment.*

SENTENCES AND PARAGRAPHS

It makes a statement in the first sentence, gives a supporting example in the second and backs up this example with fact in the third.

A paragraph will also work well if you can link its component sentences and relate them to the main point you are making. One good way of doing this is to number the different supporting points which supplement the main argument of the paragraph.

This paragraph consists of a main point and several supporting points, but they do not mesh together smoothly:

> *Our range of partitions offers clear advantages over other, similar systems. It is particularly suited to swimming-pool changing rooms: every element is water-resistant and will not degrade in a wet environment. It is vandal-resistant and can withstand hammer and knife attack. It is available in a range of colours and finishes to suit even the most adventurous design scheme.*

Now see how you can help the reader to understand your argument more clearly by adding words which number the different supporting points:

> *Our range of partitions offers clear advantages over other, similar systems. **Firstly**, it is particularly suited to swimming-pool changing rooms: every element is water-resistant and will not degrade in a wet environment. **Secondly**, it is vandal-resistant and can withstand hammer and knife attack. And, **finally**, it is available in a range of colours and finishes to suit even the most adventurous design scheme.*

An alternative way of making the sentences flow together more smoothly is to use conjunctions to link the sentences:

> Our range of partitions offers clear advantages
> over other, similar systems. It is particularly suited
> to swimming-pool changing rooms: every element
> is water-resistant and will not degrade in a wet
> environment. **In addition**, it is vandal-resistant and
> can withstand hammer and knife attack. It is **also**
> available in a range of colours and finishes to suit
> even the most adventurous design scheme.

Finally, adding a comment or a summary as the final sentence
finishes a paragraph with a flourish and gives it impact, as in the
following example:

> Our range of partitions offers clear advantages over
> other, similar systems. Firstly, it is particularly suited
> to swimming-pool changing rooms: every element
> is water-resistant and will not degrade in a wet
> environment. Secondly, it is vandal-resistant and can
> withstand hammer and knife attack. And, finally, it
> is available in a range of colours and finishes to suit
> even the most adventurous design scheme. In short,
> it combines style, strength and long-term use.

SENTENCES AND PARAGRAPHS

Checklist

- A sentence needs to stand on its own: it needs at least a subject and a finite verb.
- A fragment or support unit cannot stand by itself: it needs to be joined to a main clause or a control unit.
- Try to keep most sentences under 20 words, but allow the occasional longer sentence for variety.
- Never join short sentences together to make longer sentences simply by using a comma: you need a conjunction.
- Prefer active to passive sentences unless you have a good reason for using the passive.
- Paragraphs are simply structures to help guide the reader through your text.
- Aim for two to four sentences in each paragraph.

Clear and effective writing

Good written communication depends on the words and phrases you use. Clarity and impact are significantly improved by taking care with your vocabulary. In addition, by cutting out nonsense and pomposity, you can win your readers over more successfully. This section looks at different ways of making your writing clearer and more effective.

The best word for the job

Choosing the right word makes your writing more powerful, and helps you communicate more clearly. Always think about the specific words you choose. Don't make the mistake of using a longer word just because you think it will help you to appear clever and sophisticated: in fact, it may simply alienate the reader.

Look at this list of pairs of words. Each pair has the same meaning, but the words in the first column are more complicated, while those in the second column are simpler. There is a time and place for both, but if in doubt use the simple word:

accomplish	do
additional	more
advantageous	helpful
anticipate	expect
apparent	clear
benefit	help
capability	ability
component	part
concerning	about
contains	has

$\Rightarrow$

demonstrate	show
desire	want
determine	decide
employ	use
establish	prove
evident	clear
fabricate	make
facilitate	help
finalize	finish
impacted	affected
implement	carry out
modify	change
perform	do
permit	let
possess	own
proceed	start
provide	give
purchase	buy
require	need
reside	live
submit	hand over
transmit	send
utilize	use
verify	confirm

Practice exercise

Use simpler words in the following sentences. Check your answers on pages 184–5.

1 *I telephoned you concerning the folder I purchased from you, and which I need to submit to my committee tomorrow.*

2 *It would be advantageous for us to finalize the project: we can modify it at a date to be determined later.*

3 *They transmitted the invoice by fax, with additional information, but it was evident they hadn't implemented the changes.*

4 *It would be of benefit to us if you could perform the repairs by employing the latest components.*

5 *The holidays impacted on our plans but this demonstrated we needed additional staff.*

Jargon

Jargon refers to words or expressions used by particular groups of people or professions. It is therefore something which may not always be out of place in business English. The crucial point to consider is whether the reader will understand the jargon you might be tempted to use.

If you are writing for people who work in the same industry as you, then jargon can be extremely useful: your readers will understand it and you can communicate effectively. But if your readers won't understand it – or if you are in any doubt whether they will – then do not use jargon terms. If you are writing for a mixed audience, then use technical terms with care. It may be a good idea to provide definitions of technical terms in a glossary.

Every industry has its own jargon. For example, it is perfectly acceptable within the railway industry to talk about a *clockface timetable.* For people within the industry, this is a very neat way of expressing a well-established concept (it means that trains are always at the same minutes before or after the hour). To anyone outside the industry, however, the term is meaningless and would need a full explanation.

Perhaps the most pervasive examples of jargon come from the IT industry. This jargon-filled paragraph comes from a technical article:

> *When callers telephoned the 0990 number, they were routed via DSN to the BT Bristol exchange. Here*

> *they were connected via a CAM switch to Callnet's*
> *automated call bureau in Swindon. They were*
> *initially met with carefully-scripted IVR.*

Because this article was intended to be read by telecommunications professionals, the use of jargon was acceptable. What is less acceptable is the leaking out of jargon into non-technical situations.

Slang, buzzwords and clichés

While there may sometimes be a place for jargon in business, there are some types of language you should always try to avoid:

- **Slang** originates from groups of people who are outside the mainstream of society or see themselves as different in some way. Occasionally slang words become accepted as standard (for example *posh* and *donkey* were once considered slang), but mostly they stay outside the vocabulary suitable for business English.

- **Buzzwords** are words which are used to falsely impress. They often borrow from jargon: many of them have been imported from the IT industry. Examples include *bandwidth*, *ballpark figure*, *best of breed*, etc.

- **Clichés** are hackneyed phrases or expressions which are mostly superfluous and meaningless. Phrases such as *at the end of the day*, *when all is said and done* and *in terms of* have no place in clear English.

The hit list

Here are some examples of jargon, slang, buzzwords and clichés that you should try to avoid. In many cases they can be replaced with a simple alternative:

all things considered	in short
at this moment in time	now
backlash	reaction, counterattack
ballpark figure	estimate

→

bandwidth	capacity, resources
best of breed	best, leading
bleeding edge	the most advanced
blend together	blend
blue-sky thinking	original thinking
bulletize	use bullets
clamp down	tighten up on
crackdown	attack
crunch	crisis
customer-centric	putting the customer first
cutting edge	very advanced
de-risk	remove the risk
downsize	reduce in size
drill down	look at in more detail
fact of the matter	the main point
fighting for his life	critically ill or injured
go the whole nine yards	go beyond expectations
helicopter view	an overview
human capital	staff
in respect of	about
in terms of	for
last but not least	last
link together	link
mission-critical	essential
move the goalposts	change the requirements
plug and play	plug in and it's ready for use
put on the back burner	postpone
reinventing the wheel	unnecessary repetition of work
quantum leap	significant step

remuneration package	salary and other benefits
re-skilling	retraining
restructuring	making redundancies
singing from the same hymn sheet	in agreement
skill set	skills
state of the art	latest
take offline	discuss on another occasion
thinking outside the box	lateral thinking
water under the bridge	in the past

The following words can usually be left out altogether without affecting the meaning:

> actually
> as a matter of fact
> at the end of the day
> basically
> in actual fact
> in point of fact
> to all intents and purposes
> to be fair
> when all's said and done

Tautology, pleonasm and redundancy

The word *tautology* refers to using a word which repeats the meaning of another word in the sentence. The word *pleonasm* refers to using more words than are needed in a sentence.

Both are examples of *redundancy* – padding out writing with words that only waste the reader's time. For the sake of clear writing, both need to be eliminated. So always read what you have written carefully, word for word, to check for any infection – and eliminate these immediately.

Here are some examples of redundancies which can creep into business English:

> absolute truth (something is either the truth or it isn't)
>
> actual fact (a fact is always a fact)
>
> added bonus (a bonus is always something extra or added)
>
> advance notice (notice is always in advance)
>
> ATM machine (ATM means automated teller machine: the word 'machine' isn't needed)
>
> basic principle (principles are always basic)
>
> cancel out ('cancel' by itself means the same thing)
>
> close proximity ('proximity' means something is close: you don't need both words)
>
> currently pending (if something is pending, it's pending now)
>
> divide up ('up' isn't needed and adds nothing to the meaning)
>
> end result (the result is always at the end)
>
> established facts (facts are incontrovertible and established)
>
> essential prerequisite (these two words mean the same thing)
>
> first began (the time something began is always the first time)
>
> foreign imports (imports are always from other countries)
>
> forward planning (can you plan backwards?)
>
> free gift (gifts are always free)
>
> future prospects (prospects are always in the future)
>
> general consensus (consensus means 'agreement by all'; the word 'general' isn't needed)
>
> grateful thanks (can thanks be anything but grateful?)

$\Rightarrow$

CLEAR AND EFFECTIVE WRITING

➡️

head up (you need only say 'head')

impacted on (just use 'impacted' or 'had an effect on')

joined together (just say 'joined')

LCD display (LCD means liquid crystal display; there is no need for the word 'display')

necessary requirement (these two words mean the same thing)

new innovations (innovations are, by their very nature, new)

new starter (can you be an old starter?)

no other alternative (there is 'no other', or there is 'no alternative')

original founders (founders can't appear later on)

past history (when is history ever in the future?)

physically located ('physically' isn't needed)

PIN number (PIN means personal identification number; you don't need to say 'number' twice)

really unique, very unique (something is either unique or it's not; you can't have degrees of uniqueness)

reason why (you explain the reason or you explain why; you don't need both)

reduce down (reducing something brings it down)

still remains (simply say 'remains')

vital necessity (anything that's necessary is vital)

While we are talking about unnecessary words, it is worth noting the two overused words *situation* and *problem*. These are often misused in sentences such as these:

There is an ongoing crisis situation.

He has an ongoing injury problem.

In both cases, redundant words can be eliminated to leave something much simpler and clearer:

There's a crisis.

He has an injury.

Practice exercise

Cut out the redundancies in the following sentences. Check your answers on page 185.

1 *Entrance is restricted to ticket-holders only: the reason is because of lack of forward planning caused by the ongoing crisis situation.*
2 *In past history, new innovations have been an essential prerequisite.*
3 *There is no other alternative. The general consensus is that future prospects will divide up the nation.*
4 *The free gift was an added bonus; we offered our grateful thanks.*
5 *Everyone was unanimous: the plate was quite perfect.*

Put the action into the verb

A common source of redundancy in language is the use of a noun to do the work of a verb. This is called 'nominalization'. Look at these examples:

> *The proposal was given as a submission to the management team.*

> *We believe she took the decision to go.*

The phrases *given as a submission* and *took the decision* in fact mean *submitted* and *decided* respectively. In each case, the writer has made a noun do the work of a verb. By making a verb do its proper job – which is to describe the action – we can make the sentences shorter and clearer:

CLEAR AND EFFECTIVE WRITING

The proposal was submitted to the management team.

We believe she decided to go.

This device of putting the action into a noun instead of a verb is often used because it seems to have more weight and dignity. It doesn't: it simply uses several words when one will do.

Here are some more examples of nominalization. In each case it would be neater to use a simple verb:

to make advancement	to advance
to make an agreement	to agree
to give consideration to	to consider
to make delivery of	to deliver
to carry out evaluations	to evaluate
to give an indication of	to indicate
to carry out a launch	to launch
to make a proposition	to propose
to make reductions	to reduce
to make recommendations	to recommend
to make a resolution	to resolve
to find a solution to	to solve
to have a tendency to	to tend to

Practice exercise

Make the following sentences clearer. Check your answers on page 185.

1 *We know that he will make delivery of the package on Tuesday.*
2 *When we met with him, he put in a proposition to change the name.*
3 *With effect from today's date, all ideas should be made as submissions to the management team.*
4 *The team then held a discussion about seating arrangements.*

5 *Callit carried out the launch of the new product in Amsterdam.*

Avoid turning nouns into verbs

The reverse of the technique of nominalization is to take a normal noun and turn it into a verb, as in these examples:

> *They were incentivized to improve performance.*
>
> *They localized their sales force.*
>
> *They positioned themselves for takeover.*

Some people think that putting more meaning into verbs in this way makes a business communication sound more dynamic, but in practice it is simply irritating. Your writing will be clearer if you avoid it:

> *They were offered incentives to improve performance.*
>
> *They located their sales force in the area.*
>
> *They improved their position to prepare for takeover.*

Pompous language

The temptation to turn nouns into verbs is just one example of the pompous language that can infect business writing. There are certain phrases you would never use when you speak, and these should certainly never be used when you write. Here are some examples:

> *As of May 1st, we shall increase prices by 10 per cent.*
>
> *We are in receipt of your letter.*

What you really mean is:

> *We shall increase prices by 10 per cent from May 1st.*
>
> *We have received your letter.*

CLEAR AND EFFECTIVE WRITING

Think about the words you use and always consider whether they make your writing unnecessarily stuffy. A good start is to avoid the following expressions – they can usually be expressed in simpler terms:

and also	and
as to whether	whether
at this moment in time	now
because of the fact that	because
have the ability to	are able to
in the event that	if
is located	is
meet with	meet
on a daily basis	daily
outside of	outside
owing to the fact that	because
prior to	before
take control of	control
we have in place with	we have with
with a view to	to
with effect from today's date	from today

Ambiguity and lack of clarity

The whole point of communication is that the person at the other end receives a clear picture of what you have in your mind. Careless and sloppy writing can lead to ambiguity (where the reader might take a different message from the one you want to send) or lack of clarity (where the reader isn't clear what is going on at all). To avoid this, it is a good idea to read over your work to make sure it really says what you mean it to say.

Look at the following example:

> *A piano is being sold by a lady with carved legs.*

CLEAR AND EFFECTIVE WRITING

Undoubtedly the lady doesn't really have carved legs, but that is what the sentence seems to be saying. There are several clearer ways of getting the meaning across:

> *A piano with carved legs is being sold by a lady.*

> *A piano, which has carved legs, is being sold by a lady.*

> *A lady is selling a carved-leg piano.*

There is also ambiguity in this sentence:

> *The committee made recommendations for educational reforms in 2007.*

What does the writer mean to say? Does 'in 2007' refer to when the committee made its recommendations, or to when the reforms would be carried out? A more thoughtful sentence structure can make this clear:

> *In 2007, the committee made recommendations for educational reforms.*

> *The committee made recommendations for educational reforms to take place in 2007.*

Always make sure that the words in a sentence are in the most helpful order. Here's another example:

> *Working in both a business environment and studying has given me great experience.*

The careless positioning of the word *both* means that the sentence is actually saying *Working in a business environment and working in studying.* This is nonsensical. But more careful arrangement of the words makes the meaning clear:

> *Both working in a business environment and studying have given me great experience.*

CLEAR AND EFFECTIVE WRITING

Follow these tips to help you avoid ambiguity in your writing:

* Be aware of the potential for ambiguity to creep into your writing: read it and think if it is really saying what you want it to say.
* Use simple and clear sentence structures.
* If your meaning isn't clear, then add in details to improve clarity.
* Don't assume your reader will understand: if in doubt, change it.
* Show your writing to someone else: they may have a different way of interpreting what you have written.

Checklist

* Stick to simple words.
* Avoid jargon, slang, buzzwords and clichés.
* Don't use several words where one will do.
* Use verbs rather than nouns to describe action.
* Don't use words because you think they sound impressive: this just makes you sound pompous.
* Read your writing through or get a colleague to read it through to check it is clear and not ambiguous.

Common misunderstandings

There are a number of rules of English grammar which have become fixed in many people's minds. It may be that your ability to write clearly is restricted by worrying about breaking these rules. In fact, some of these supposed rules are not true. In this section we'll look at some of the myths about grammar. Some pedants may take issue with you over them and you can use this section to state your case – and with any luck win the argument!

It is OK to start a sentence with *And*

There is nothing wrong with starting a sentence with *And* – and in fact it can really help your writing.

Compare these two paragraphs:

> *This breakthrough harnesses our unique technology, which draws on an everyday principle of how light travels through glass. We've applied this to develop a touchscreen which eliminates the need for special glass, coatings, moving parts or exposed elements. Our screens will also continue to perform even in the harshest environments, ensuring maximum return on investment.*

> *This breakthrough harnesses our unique technology, which draws on an everyday principle of how light travels through glass. We've applied this to develop a touchscreen which eliminates the need for special glass, coatings, moving parts or exposed elements.* **And our screens** *will continue to perform even in the harshest environments, ensuring maximum return on investment.*

COMMON MISUNDERSTANDINGS

There is nothing wrong with the first example. But in the second example the use of *And* to introduce the final sentence builds the advantages and presses the final point home more firmly. And it's not grammatically incorrect.

It is OK to start a sentence with *But*

It is perfectly correct to start a sentence with *But* – and it gives you extra options which can make your writing more interesting.

Look at the following example:

> *The changing rooms are on the side of the pool, which makes them convenient for users. This means, of course, that they are more exposed to the humidity and chemicals common in pool environments and which can affect many conventional cubicle elements.* **But not now**: *the Marathon system has been specifically designed to overcome this.*

Using *But* to start the sentence creates a dramatic impact and really presses the point home – and it's not grammatically incorrect.

It is OK to start a sentence with *However*

You can start a sentence with *However*, as in the following example:

> *We would take the burden of administration for the scheme: application form creation, form sifting, applicant contact, liaison with judges, etc, so please don't worry about it causing a lot of extra work for you and your team.* **However**, *we would of course keep you involved and would like to involve you in strategic decisions and planning at every stage.*

Using *However* at the beginning of the sentence makes the point more firmly than if the word were moved to the middle of a sentence:

We would of course keep you involved, however, and would like to involve you in strategic decisions and planning at every stage.

It is OK to split an infinitive

The best-known example of a split infinitive comes from the television series *Star Trek:*

To boldly go where no man has gone before.

The infinitive form of a verb is the form that has the word 'to' in front of it – in this case *to go*. The word *boldly* splits *to go*, creating a so-called 'split infinitive'. Purists argue that this should never happen, but there is no reason why. The basis of their assertion comes from Latin grammar, where the infinitive comprises a single word and cannot be split. But English is not Latin.

Sometimes a split infinitive can actually help the sense of the sentence, as in this example where the infinitive *to triple* is split:

The company wants to more than triple the number of staff over ten months.

Some might argue that, as there are people who hate seeing a split infinitive, you should avoid the structure in case it offends your readers. A sensible course is only to allow split infinitives if you can't find a suitable alternative way of saying what you mean.

It is OK to have a comma in front of *and*

A comma before the word *and* is perfectly acceptable and indeed can help to emphasize your meaning. This point will be dealt with on page 49.

You can end a sentence with a preposition

A preposition is something that links one word – usually a noun or pronoun – with another: examples are *on*, *with*, *after*, *for* and *in*.

COMMON MISUNDERSTANDINGS

Some people object to sentences such as these:

> *This is something we must invest in.*

> *He admired some of the campaigns I worked on.*

Purists would argue that this should be rewritten as:

> *This is something in which we must invest.*

> *He admired some of the campaigns on which I worked.*

The problem with adopting this rule can be seen if you try to rework a sentence such as this one:

> *She had forgotten which page she was up to.*

Following the commonly held belief, this would have to be written thus:

> *She had forgotten up to which page she was.*

As this example shows, sometimes a sentence just doesn't work unless the preposition *is* at the end of the sentence. In short, there's nothing wrong with this type of sentence structure: if it reads well, use it; if it doesn't, turn it around.

Good punctuation

Using the right punctuation makes what you are trying to say clear – and increases the chance of your reader understanding your writing the first time they read it. This section is designed to give you an overview of how to use different punctuation marks correctly.

Apostrophes

To illustrate how important an apostrophe can be in communicating what you really mean, look at these words:

> *ill, shell, well, hell, were*

It's perfectly clear what these words mean. But if you add an apostrophe, the meaning changes completely:

> *I'll (I will), she'll (she will), we'll (we will), he'll (he will), we're (we are)*

Now look at these phrases:

> *the bands on stage*
>
> *the band's on stage*

In the first example, without the apostrophe, *bands* is a plural and refers to more than one band being on the stage at that time. In the second example, *band's* is a contraction of *band is* and refers to one band.

These examples all demonstrate that an apostrophe is not an optional extra: it is needed to make your writing communicate exactly what you want to say.

Uses of the apostrophe

The apostrophe has two uses:

GOOD PUNCTUATION

- to mark the omission of something
- to show that something is a possessive

Firstly, an apostrophe can be used to replace something that has been removed (one letter or several letters). Whatever remains is moved together around the apostrophe. So *it is* becomes *it's* and *who will* becomes *who'll*:

> *It's time to go home.*

> *Who'll chair the meeting?*

If you remove some numbers when writing a year or decade, you add an apostrophe:

> *the summer of '96*

> *We experienced major growth throughout the '90s.*

Secondly, an apostrophe is also used to show that something belongs to someone or something:

> *the lady's handbag* (*the handbag belonging to the lady*)

> *the boy's books* (*the books belonging to the boy*)

Note that the idea of possession is present in many phrases that indicate a period of time, such as these:

> *one week's holiday* (*a holiday of one week*)

> *two years' experience* (*the experience gained over two years*)

> *three months' notice* (*a notice period of three months*)

Positioning the apostrophe

When an apostrophe shows possession, the best way to check if you have it in the right place is to turn the sentence around. If you turn *the boy's books* around into *the books belonging to the boy*, you will then identify that you are talking about the singular noun *boy*. The apostrophe should always go after the name of the thing you are talking about:

>   *IBM's staff*   (*the staff at IBM*)
>
>   *the man's diary*   (*the diary belonging to the man*)
>
>   *the team's proposal* (*the proposal by the team*)

When the word with the apostrophe is a plural, the apostrophe should still go after the name of the thing you are talking about. Again, you can check that you have got it right by turning the sentence around:

>   *the boys' books*   (*the books belonging to the boys*)

By turning the sentence around, you can identify that you are talking about the plural noun *boys*, so this time the apostrophe needs to go after the *s*.

Remember that not all plural nouns end in *s*. With plurals such as *children* and *geese*, the apostrophe comes before the *s*:

>   *the children's department* (*the department for children*)
>
>   *the geese's eggs*   (*the eggs of the geese*)

Common misuses of the apostrophe
People who are not clear about the correct use of the apostrophe sometimes put it in places where it doesn't belong, and this can get in the way of the meaning. There are plenty of words that end in *s* that do not need an apostrophe.

Do not use an apostrophe for a verb that ends in *s*:

✔ *The window lets the light in.*

✗ *The window let's the light in.*

GOOD PUNCTUATION

Do not use an apostrophe for the simple plural form of a noun:

> ✔ *We sell pizzas.*

> ✗ *We sell pizza's.*

There is sometimes a temptation to do this with the plural forms of abbreviations and dates:

> ✔ *a superb range of CDs*

> ✗ *a superb range of CD's*

> ✔ *the 1970s*

> ✗ *the 1970's*

Plural forms of words that consist of a single letter are an exception. It is a good idea to use an apostrophe here simply to avoid confusion:

> *There are two o's and two s's in 'looses'.*

> *Mind your p's and q's.*

Another class of words that causes difficulty are the words such as *yours*, *hers* and *ours*, which are called possessive pronouns. These words – as their name suggests – already indicate possession, so they do not need an apostrophe:

> *I returned the book, which was hers.*

> *Ours is a generation which knows how to enjoy life.*

> *Whose desk needs cleaning?*

The possessive pronoun that causes most difficulty for writers is *its*. It is worth making a special effort to remember that the only time you write *it's* is when it means 'it is' or 'it has':

> ✔ *It's been a long time since I saw you.*

> ✗ *The company has lost it's way recently.*

> ✔ *The company has lost its way recently.*

Practice exercise

Put in apostrophes where needed. Check your answers on page 185.

1 *Its mother decided it was time to give its child its milk.*
2 *The lady gave some eggs and tomatoes to her childrens friends.*
3 *During the 1980s, the governments policy was to reduce its spending.*
4 *In two years time, it will have completed its term as a blind persons companion.*
5 *Its time to decide whose friend you are and whose going to go with you.*
6 *The book was theirs; it wasnt hers.*
7 *There was a months gap between its first and last win.*

Inverted commas or quotation marks

Inverted commas are used to show the beginning and end of direct speech or excerpts from other material. They come in pairs:

> *Rob Thornton said, 'Our new factory will provide significant employment for the village.'*

Inverted commas may be written as single or double marks – there is no hard-and-fast rule to follow. This is a question of taste and is often governed by your company's house style. The key is to choose one style and apply it consistently.

For clarity, never use the same style of inverted commas when you have one quotation within another: use single for the main quote and double for the secondary, or vice versa:

> *'When she screamed out "Help!", I started to get worried,' said Mike.*

> *"When she screamed out 'Help!', I started to get worried," said Mike.*

Quotation marks should enclose the exact words of the speaker. If words identifying the speaker appear in the middle, close the quotation marks and then reopen them:

GOOD PUNCTUATION

> *'Our new factory will provide significant employment for the village,' commented Rob Thornton, 'and will for many years to come.'*

The rule for placing a punctuation mark at the end of quoted speech is that, if the punctuation applies to the quote itself, it goes inside the quotation mark:

> *He remarked, 'I'm going to be only ten minutes late.'*

But if the punctuation does not apply to the quote, but rather to the whole sentence, it goes after the final quotation mark:

> *He remarked that he would be 'only ten minutes late'.*

Although quotation marks come in pairs, there is one special case: if a quote continues into another paragraph, you do not put in closing marks until the end of the complete quote. You do, however, use a quotation mark at the beginning of each new paragraph:

> *'Our new factory,' said Rob Thornton, 'will be opening in September. We are confident that this will provide significant opportunities for the village.*
>
> *'In addition, we are creating 50 new jobs in our Cardiff offices. These will bring the total staff of the company up to 460.'*

Commas

Commas are used to break up a sentence and create a pause, in a number of different ways.

A comma separates the different elements in a simple list:

> *The following items are needed: pencil, ruler, rubber, paper, highlighter and stapler.*

Notice that in this example there is no comma before the word *and*.

But a comma here can be useful if you want to separate the final item more clearly. Compare these two examples:

> *The telephone operators yawned, stretched, grimaced, coughed and squirmed with boredom.*

> *The telephone operators yawned, stretched, grimaced, coughed, and squirmed with boredom.*

In the first example, everything was caused by boredom; the final comma in the second example changes the meaning, so that only the squirming was caused by boredom.

A comma can also be used to clarify meaning. Compare the following sentences:

> *Below, the keyboard was broken.*

> *Below the keyboard was broken.*

In the first instance, the keyboard itself was broken; in the second, something else which is underneath the keyboard is broken.

Now look at the following sentence: what does it mean?

> *Shortly after the snow warning lights went out.*

Depending on where you put a comma, the meaning can change completely:

> *Shortly after, the snow warning lights went out.*

> *Shortly after the snow, warning lights went out.*

> *Shortly after the snow warning, lights went out.*

A comma can also be used to separate extra information in a sentence. A pair of commas is used to separate information which isn't absolutely essential to the sense of the sentence. These are called 'bracketing commas', and do the same work as brackets or dashes:

> *The leader, who lived in a private apartment, needed regular meetings to be kept informed.*

> *The building, which included private meeting rooms and sports facilities, was available for general use.*

In both cases, the whole phrase inside the commas could be removed and the sentence would still make sense:

> *The leader needed regular meetings to be kept informed.*

> *The building was available for general use.*

If the information is essential to the meaning, however, then it is not separated from the rest of the sentence by commas. Consider the difference between these two sentences:

> *Staff who regularly go on holiday will miss out on certain benefits.*

> *Staff, who regularly go on holiday, will miss out on certain benefits.*

In the first example, only those members of staff who regularly go on holiday will miss out on benefits. The whole phrase *Staff who regularly go on holiday* is the subject of the sentence and cannot be interrupted by a comma. But in the second example, all the staff will miss out on certain benefits, and all of them regularly go on holiday. *Staff* is the subject of the sentence, while *who regularly go on holiday* is a subordinate (supporting) unit and needs to be separated from the main part of the sentence by two commas.

If the extra information comes at the beginning or the end of a sentence, a single comma is enough to separate it from the main part of the sentence:

> *They went to the boardroom, which was on the top floor.*

> *If you don't meet the deadline, you will miss the opportunity.*

In the first sentence, *They went to the boardroom* is the main part of the sentence (the control unit); *which was on the top floor* adds extra information and could not stand alone. In the second sentence, *you will miss the opportunity* is the main part of the sentence (control unit); *If you don't meet the deadline* adds extra information and could not stand alone.

If you don't use a comma to mark off the supporting unit from the control unit, the sentence can be ambiguous or unclear:

> ✗ *As you know the management team is in the building.*

> ✔ *As you know, the management team is in the building.*

In the first sentence, the meaning is only clear once you finish reading; in the second case, the meaning is immediately clear.

A comma is used before *and* to emphasize a contrast:

> *The meeting lasted all night and part of the next day.*

> *The meeting lasted all night, and in the morning they went home.*

This use of the comma also applies to lists, where separating the final element will create a contrast:

> *The models were tall, thin, long-legged, and vastly overpaid.*

A comma can be used to mark the beginning or end of speech or a quotation in the middle of a sentence:

> *John said, 'I'll be there at eight.'*

> *'I'll be there at eight,' said John.*

GOOD PUNCTUATION

Common misuses of the comma

A comma must *never* appear between a subject and its verb:

   ✗ *John, knew he would never succeed.*

   ✔ *John knew he would never succeed.*

   ✗ *London, is the capital of England.*

   ✔ *London is the capital of England.*

If commas are used in pairs to bracket extra information, then the sentence should work if the extra information is removed:

   ✗ *She said that most, if not all of, the staff were leaving.*

If you take out the information within the commas, you are left with an incomplete fragment:

   ✗ *She said that most the staff were leaving.*

So the second comma needs to be placed more carefully:

   ✔ *She said that most, if not all, of the staff were leaving.*

Now, if you take out the information within the commas, you are left with a complete sentence:

   ✔ *She said that most of the staff were leaving.*

It is important not to leave out the second comma when you want to separate supplementary information in the middle of a sentence:

   ✗ *The product, which was selling well would now be manufactured in India.*

   ✔ *The product, which was selling well, would now be manufactured in India.*

Practice exercise

Insert commas in the right places. Check you answers on pages 185–6.

1 *The carpet which is soiled is going to be replaced.*

2 *Although they wanted to go they stayed inside.*
3 *He implied that some if not all of the proposal was wrong.*
4 *We have sent the goods although they may take time to reach you.*
5 *They held a discussion and afterwards they had a meal together.*

Colons

Colons are used to introduce things.

A common use of colons is in a two-part sentence when the second part expands on or explains a completed statement. This second part could either stand alone as a separate sentence or be a subordinate (supporting) clause:

> *Sally didn't attend the meeting: she had to fly to Glasgow.*

> *Mark shivered: a combination of nerves and the cold.*

A colon can also introduce a list, as in the following example:

> *The following areas are closed: cafeteria, library, terrace and garden.*

The most common use of colons in business English is to introduce quotations, for example in press releases:

> *Peter Smith, the chairman of Smith & Co, commented: 'This represents a major step forward for our industry.'*

> *Gemma Green, Marketing Director, is delighted with the results: 'We were convinced it would be successful and this has proved our point.'*

Practice exercise

Insert a colon in these examples. Check your answers on page 186.
1 *Chris Beattie, who made the device, believes it will fill a gap in the market 'Our research shows there is considerable demand.'*
2 *The interviews were held in various rooms offices, hallways, the reception area.*

3 *David couldn't leave the office on time he needed to finish his report.*

4 *The team were devastated no orders and no prospect of any for at least a month.*

Semicolons

Whereas colons always introduce things, semicolons always connect things of equal importance. The two cannot be used interchangeably.

Semicolons can join together short sentences which, if they ran separately, might sound rather disjointed and staccato:

> *Jones sat on one side. Smith sat on the other. The document was on the table between them.*

Using semicolons, the story flows and the tension mounts:

> *Jones sat on one side; Smith sat on the other; the document was on the table between them.*

Changing the final semicolon to a full stop creates a dramatic change:

> *Jones sat on one side; Smith sat on the other. The document was on the table between them.*

Here is another example of how using semicolons can make a difference:

> *The hotel nestles in a hollow; all around are grazing sheep and cattle; trees in the distance mark out the boundaries.*

Using semicolons here makes the description flow and creates a unified picture. Using short sentences and full stops would give it a more punchy but disjointed feel:

> *The hotel nestles in a hollow. All around are grazing*

> *sheep and cattle. Trees in the distance mark out the*
> *boundaries.*

By using one full stop and one semicolon, we can shift the focus firmly to the hotel and its location:

> *The hotel nestles in a hollow. All around are grazing*
> *sheep and cattle; trees in the distance mark out the*
> *boundaries.*

Another use of the semicolon is to bring together two statements which, when joined, create a balance:

> *The racket is short and light to use; the ball is white*
> *and easy to see.*

> *Some called him a genius; others claimed he was a*
> *fraud.*

Finally, if a list contains elements which have internal punctuation, these can be separated more clearly by using a semicolon:

> *The following elements are needed: a screen, with an*
> *anti-glare cover; a keyboard, mouse and mouse mat; a*
> *colour printer, with or without paper; and speakers.*

If commas were used to separate the elements, the list would be very confusing:

> ✗ *The following elements are needed: a screen, with an anti-*
> *glare cover, a keyboard, mouse and mouse mat, a colour*
> *printer, with or without paper and speakers.*

Practice exercise

Change these sentences to include semicolons. Check your answers on page 186.

1 *Peter wanted to pay the full amount. John did not. An argument*
   ensued.
2 *The course comprised a number of units: elementary English,*

including punctuation, clear writing, with lots of exercises, and practical exercises.

3 *The screen is bright and clear. The keyboard is small and compact.*

Exclamation marks

Perhaps the last word on exclamation marks was written by H W Fowler, who observed that using them excessively is 'a certain indication of an unpractised writer or of one who wants to add a spurious dash of sensation to something unsensational'.

In short, exclamation marks should be used with caution. They look unprofessional and are rarely used in business English – even in e-mails.

Brackets

Brackets are used to separate words from the rest of a sentence. This is usually either to provide extra information or to show options, as in these examples:

> *It was one of the earliest finds (London, 1645).*

> *She returned the car (a Citröen Estate) to the showroom.*

> *Look out for the best restaurants (like the Café Royal, which has a great reputation).*

> *The report showed quite clearly (page 200, line 6) that it was true.*

In all these cases, the words in the brackets could be dropped and would leave a perfectly complete sentence. They simply add more information and colour.

Brackets can be useful as they allow you to accommodate a range of possibilities without having to tailor your writing to each specific case:

Your letter(s) will be returned.

Your child (children) should arrive at 10am.

Square brackets may be used if you need an additional set of brackets within brackets:

The report presented evidence about the disaster (and its aftermath [reported below]).

Square brackets can also be used to add information which is needed to make the sense clear:

Business to business is not in our plans [for new business] but we never say never.

They may also be used in business documents to indicate a change to the original:

*The **very best seat** [format added] was given away.*

Practice exercise

Insert round or square brackets as appropriate. Check your answers on page 186.

1 *The shop Choc a Lot was closed on Fridays.*
2 *We looked at it the estate and decided to buy.*
3 *The loaf loaves must then be left in the oven for 10 minutes.*
4 *The gallery contained the finest examples of Impressionist art Monet, Gauguin, Degas.*

Dashes

A dash can create dramatic effect. It creates more of a pause than using a comma:

Everyone expected a pay rise – but not as much as 50 per cent.

The curtain went back and there she stood – totally naked.

> *It seemed the best product for us – after they'd reduced the price.*

A pair of dashes can be used to separate extra information within a sentence. A pair of dashes does the same work as a pair of brackets or commas:

> *He got together his things – pencil, ruler, rubber, pen and ink – and started the exam.*

> *He returned the car – a Citröen Estate – to the showroom.*

Note that the dash should not be used to do the work of a colon:

> ✗ *The place was devastated – trees uprooted; windows broken; tiles on the ground.*

> ✔ *The place was devastated: trees uprooted; windows broken; tiles on the ground.*

Practice exercise

Insert a dash where needed. Check your answers on page 186.

1 *He knew he had won but not by that much.*
2 *The team knew the prospective customer a tough operator would be difficult to win over.*
3 *She had seen him before and talked to him without permission.*
4 *They collected the materials wire, connectors, plugs and brackets and started to put them together.*

Hyphens

Some words that are created by combining two shorter words are always hyphenated. Here are some examples:

> *close-knit*

> *closed-circuit*

> *co-op*

> *co-worker*

cross-country

do-it-yourself

fine-drawn

flip-flop

front-end

know-all

Hyphens are also used to join words together to remove ambiguity from written English. Take this famous example:

man-eating dog seen in park

man eating dog seen in park

With the hyphen, it is clear that the dog is prone to eating humans; without the hyphen, it is clear that the man is prone to eating dogs. So, if two words jointly describe another word and would cause confusion if left separate, then use a hyphen:

highest-quality service

red-haired girl

two-year sentence

low-key approach

Common mistakes

The English language is full of words which are almost identical in their spelling but have completely different definitions. There are also other words which, through overfamiliarity, have come to be used incorrectly. Using these carelessly can render your writing ridiculous and undermine its value.

This section looks at these easily confused words. At the end there is an extended exercise to help you check your knowledge.

adverse, averse

Adverse means unfortunate or unfavourable:

> *There are adverse weather conditions.*

Averse means unwilling:

> *He was not averse to helping me.*

advertise, improvise, supervise, televise

These words are always spelt with an *s*, even if you choose to use a *z* as the standard spelling for words such as *apologize*, *capitalize*, *criticize*, etc.

advice, advise

Advice is a noun:

> *We gave them our considered advice.*

Advise is a verb:

> *We will advise them to reduce the price.*

affect, effect

Affect is a verb. It means to alter, to attack, to move emotionally:

> *He tried to affect the result.*

> *She affected him so much he stopped running.*

It can also mean to pretend:

> *He affected indifference to her feelings.*

Effect is a noun. The effect of something is its result, consequence or impression:

> *The customer contact programme had a significant effect on the sales of the product.*

> *The red lights created a stunning effect.*

It has other uses, although these can make your writing stiff and formal:

> *With effect from today's date* (much better to say *From today*)

> *The change gave effect to a major debate.* (much better to say *The change caused a major debate.*)

However, *effect* can also be a verb, meaning to accomplish or bring about:

> *The government effected great changes.*

allusion, illusion, allude, elude

An *allusion* is a passing reference:

> *He made an allusion to Shakespeare.*

An *illusion* is something that doesn't exist:

> *He thought he saw a ghost but it was an illusion.*

COMMON MISTAKES

To *allude* means to refer to something:

> *He alluded to it in his speech.*

To *elude* means to avoid something:

> *He eluded capture and managed to reach safety.*

alternative, choice

You have an *alternative* of two things; you can have a *choice* of any number:

> *The alternatives were either to drive or to walk.*

> *He had a choice between walking or driving.*

> *He had a choice between walking, driving and cycling.*

amend, emend

There is a subtle difference between these two words. To *amend* means to make changes or improve:

> *He amended the proposal to include costs and timings.*

To *emend* means to remove errors:

> *He emended the letter so that it was perfect.*

amid, amidst

Either of these words is acceptable. In the interests of clear English, however, use *amid*: it sounds more modern and less pretentious than *amidst*.

among, amongst

As with *amid* and *amidst*, either of these words is acceptable. In the interests of clear English, however, use *among*: it sounds more modern and less pretentious than *amongst*.

appraise, apprise

To *appraise* means to evaluate:

>   *I appraised his performance.*

To *apprise* means to inform:

>   *I apprised him of his progress, pointing out areas for improvement.*

assure, ensure, insure

To *assure* means to promise or give your word:

>   *I can assure you I am telling the truth.*

To *ensure* means to make certain:

>   *They will ensure you reach your destination safely.*

To *insure* means to take out a policy with an insurance company:

>   *You can insure your property against theft.*

aural, oral

aural means listening or by ear:

>   *They listened to a CD during their aural examination.*

oral refers to the mouth or speaking:

>   *The French oral involved 30 minutes' conversation.*

bait, bated

You use *bait* to trap something:

>   *The bait was hidden by the long grass.*

Bated means held back:

>   *He waited with bated breath.*

COMMON MISTAKES

canvas, canvass

Canvas is a material:

> *The seat was covered in canvas.*

To *canvass* is to solicit votes or research:

> *He will canvass for the candidate in the local election.*

censor, censure

A *censor* is someone who checks material for standards or harmful material; *to censor* is to carry out this task:

> *Mail from high-security prisoners is carefully censored.*

To *censure* means to criticize:

> *The witness was censured for deliberately misleading the jury.*

cite, sight, site

To *cite* means to refer to or to mention:

> *The company was cited in the court case.*

A *sight* is something you see:

> *It was a sight for sore eyes.*

A *site* is a place:

> *The site was flat and perfect for the structure.*

compare with, compare to

You use *compare with* when you want to stress the difference between two things:

> *She compares extremely well with her sister.*

> *That compares favourably with this.*

> *His achievements cannot compare with those of his father.*

You use *compare to* when you want to stress similarity:

> *He compared the landscape to a painting.*

> *He compared my singing to Robbie Williams'.*

complacent, complaisant

If you are *complacent*, you are self-satisfied:

> *The others presented well so we shouldn't be complacent about winning the contract.*

If you are *complaisant*, you want to please someone or something:

> *She was very complaisant in her manner: she would do anything to make him like her.*

complement, compliment

Complement and *complementary* refer to something that matches, goes with or is complete:

> *The range included letter-headings and complementary envelopes.*

A *compliment* is something nice that you say about someone; *complimentary* means 'free of charge':

> *She paid him a compliment to make him feel better.*

> *Entrance is complimentary, to show our appreciation.*

Mistaking these two words can actually cause commercial problems, as in this example:

> ✗ *Special offer: high-speed kettle. Also available: complimentary iron.*

COMMON MISTAKES

The word *complimentary* means that the iron is available free of charge – which may not be what the writer intended.

continual, continuous

If something is *continual*, it happens at regular intervals:

> *The heckler butted in continually during the speech.*

If something is *continuous*, it never stops:

> *It rained continuously from dawn until dusk.*

copyright, copywriting

Copyright is the legal protection given to the creators of an artistic work.

Copywriting (which is carried out by copywriters) is the work of writing an advert or a brochure:

> *The copywriting will be finished tomorrow and then we can go ahead with design.*

could have, could've, could of

Could've is a contraction of *could have*. When it is spoken, it sounds a little like *could of* and therefore it is sometimes (mistakenly) written in this way.

Never, ever use *could of*. In business English, you are unlikely to use the contraction *could've*. The same applies to *must have*, *should have*, *might have*, *will have*, etc.

council, counsel

A *council* is a group of people, often elected. Its members are *councillors*:

> *The council meets on Thursdays.*

Counsel is advice. The people who dispense it are *counsellors*:

> *The counsel he gave me was invaluable.*

criterion, criteria

Criterion is the singular form; *criteria* is the plural:

> *The criterion for selection was that they were able to sell.*

> *The criteria for selection are selling skills, writing skills and a pleasant personality.*

decimate

To *decimate* literally means 'to reduce by one tenth' but has come to mean 'to partially destroy or debilitate'; it does not mean 'to completely obliterate':

> *The company was decimated by the redundancies: the remaining workforce found it hard to cope.*

despite, in spite of

There is no difference between *despite* and *in spite of*: they both mean *even though*. In the spirit of clear and concise English, use *despite* as it comprises fewer words.

different from, different to

Different from is the commonly accepted form; *different to* is more colloquial. *Different than* should never be used.

defuse, diffuse

To *defuse* means to take the heat out of something:

> *He defused the argument by changing the subject.*

To *diffuse* means to spread out or disperse:

> *The impact was diffused over a wide area.*

COMMON MISTAKES

dependant, dependent

Dependant is a noun and means someone who relies on someone else:

> *He has three dependants living with him.*

Dependent is an adjective:

> *He's dependent on his father for money.*

disc, disk

Disk is a computer term:

> *Please insert the floppy disk into the drive.*

Disc is used in all other instances:

> *compact disc*
>
> *disc brake*

discreet, discrete

Discreet means guarded, careful or prudent:

> *She was asked to be discreet when explaining about the redundancies.*

Discrete means separate, apart or detached:

> *The garage was discrete from the house.*

disinterested, uninterested

If you are *disinterested*, you have no involvement or are impartial:

> *Judges are supposed to be disinterested in the cases they try.*

If you are *uninterested*, you are bored or unenthusiastic:

> *Jane was quite uninterested in the football.*

effective, efficient

If something is *effective*, it achieves what is required; if something is *efficient*, it happens in an organized and timely manner. So something can be both efficient and effective, as in this example:

> *The new service help desk provides a more efficient service which will be more effective in solving customer complaints.*

elicit, illicit

To *elicit* means to draw something out or obtain:

> *They will elicit a warm response if it all goes to plan.*

Illicit means illegal:

> *They won through illicit entries.*

eminent, immanent, imminent

Someone who is *eminent* is well-known or distinguished:

> *The eminent surgeon Cathy Brook will discuss procedures on Thursday.*

If something is *immanent* it is inherent or inborn:

> *It was immanent in him and he couldn't stop himself from doing it.*

If something is *imminent*, it is about to happen:

> *The storm was imminent: the clouds were almost black.*

evoke, invoke

To *evoke* means to stir up, to suggest or to remind:

> *The results evoked a storm of protest from shareholders.*

COMMON MISTAKES

To *invoke* means to bring into play:

> If necessary, we shall invoke the penalty clause and start legal proceedings.

farther, further

Farther and *further* are interchangeable when used to indicate distance:

> Bristol is farther away than Swindon.

> London is further away than Reading.

They are not interchangeable when used to mean 'additional':

> The board demanded further staff reductions.

faze, phase

To *faze* means to confuse, shock or upset:

> They were fazed by the size of the losses.

A *phase* is a period of time:

> The campaign will comprise three phases: approaching prospective customers; following up strong leads; and cold calling.

factious, fractious

Factious means 'divisive or likely to split into factions':

> The village was in turmoil after a factious election campaign.

Fractious means 'irritable or restless':

> The children were fractious because they were hungry.

flammable, inflammable, non-flammable

If something is *flammable*, it can catch fire; *inflammable* also means it can catch fire; *non-flammable* means it cannot catch fire:

*It was an inflammable liquid so it needed to be kept
away from bright sunlight.*

*The material is non-flammable so can be used for
children's clothing.*

flair, flare

Someone who has a *flair* has a talent:

The whole team showed a flair for creativity.

A *flare* is a large candle:

They lit the flare to signal to the search party.

Flares are wide-bottomed trousers:

He had flared trousers.

flaunt, flout

To *flaunt* means to display openly:

He flaunted his experience to impress them.

To *flout* means to ignore or defy:

He flouted the conventions and didn't wear a tie.

forego, forgo

To *forego* means to go in front of something:

It was a foregone conclusion.

To *forgo* means to go without something:

I think I will forgo the pudding.

himself, herself, yourself

Words such as *himself*, *herself* and *yourself* are purely used for
emphasis:

> *He did the painting himself!*
>
> *I went there myself.*

They are not interchangeable with *me, you, him, her*, etc:

✗ *I will meet with yourself next week.*

✗ *You gave it to myself.*

historic, historical

Historic is used to describe something which is likely to be of lasting significance:

> *It was a historic occasion: the first time a woman had entered the House of Commons.*

Historical is used to describe something in history:

> *Jesus was a historical figure.*

hoard, horde

To *hoard* means to hide away or something secreted:

> *He hoards chocolate.*
>
> *He had a hoard of chocolate.*

A *horde* is a crowd or a flock:

> *There were hordes of shareholders at the meeting.*

hopefully

Hopefully is an adverb which means 'full of hope':

> *She sat there hopefully, waiting for him to arrive.*

Many people object to the use of *hopefully* to mean 'it is hoped', so you need to be cautious about this use:

> *Hopefully the sun will shine on Sunday.*

I, me

For some reason, many people believe it is incorrect English ever to say ...*and me*. It is not.

The use of *I* and *me* therefore causes many mistakes, but in fact has a very simple rule: *I* is used for the subject of the verb; otherwise *me* is used. These examples illustrate the point:

> *I walk down the street.* (*I* is the subject of *walk*)

> *John walks down the street with me.* (*Me* is not the subject of *walk*)

The confusion comes when *me* is used with another name: but in fact this does not change the rule. Using *me* after the word *and* is perfectly correct:

> *John and I walked down the street.* (*John* and *I* are the subject of *walk*)

> *John walked down the street with Jane and me.* (*Jane* and *me* are not the subject of *walk*)

Do not be tempted to write this:

> ✗ *John walked down the street with Jane and I.*

lead, led

Lead is the present tense of the verb which means 'to be at the front of':

> *I lead from the front now – it's my new style.*

Lead is also a metal:

> *She has shares in a lead mine.*

Led is the past tense of the verb *to lead*:

> *I led the meeting on the first three occasions; on the*

fourth, it was led by John.

less, fewer

Although you will have undoubtedly been in a supermarket and seen a sign at the checkout saying, 'Nine items or less', this is not correct English.

Less is the comparative of the word *little*; *fewer* is the comparative of the word *few*. The two do not mean the same thing. The key is whether the meaning involves something which is countable or not:

> *Schumacher took on less fuel than Button.*
>
> *Schumacher took on fewer gallons of fuel than Button.*

In the first example, *fuel* isn't something you can count and therefore the correct word is *less*; in the second example, *gallons* are countable, and so the correct word to use is *fewer*.

These two sentences show how the difference between *less* and *fewer* changes the sense:

> *The less people know, the better.*
>
> *The fewer people know, the better.*

In the first example, people are given less information. In the second, there is a smaller number of people who know about it.

Exactly the same rules apply to *least* and *fewest*.

licence, license

Licence is the noun; *license* is the verb:

> *He had a licence to sell alcohol.*
>
> *He is licensed to sell alcohol.*
>
> *James Bond has a licence to kill.*

loose, lose

If something is *loose*, it is not tight:

> *The arrangement was rather loose and we had plenty of room for manoeuvre.*

To *lose* something is to misplace it:

> *We're going to lose the contract if we don't start performing.*

luxuriant, luxurious

If something is *luxuriant*, it is prolific or growing profusely:

> *He has luxuriant hair.*

If something is *luxurious*, it offers a great deal of comfort:

> *The hotel was luxurious.*

meet, mete out

To *meet* means to come together in one place:

> *I will meet him tomorrow.*

To *mete* means to apportion or allot:

> *He meted out punishment to the children.*

meter, metre

Meters are machines which measure:

> *the electricity meter*

Metres are units of measurement:

> *The pool is three metres deep at one end.*

militate, mitigate

To *militate* means to have an effect on; it is usually followed by *against*:

> *Their new product militates against our drive to increase sales.*

To *mitigate* means to make less intense or to alleviate:

> *The wall will mitigate the effects of the tide.*

none

None is always used with a singular verb:

✔ *None of the employees is happy with their pay rise.*

✗ *None of the employees are happy with their pay rise.*

passed, past

Passed is the past tense of the verb *to pass*:

> *She passed all her exams.*

> *They passed the documents to the supervisor.*

Past is a preposition or adverb used to convey time or distance:

> *He hurried past the traffic lights.*

> *I looked back on past times with fondness.*

pedal, peddle

A *pedal* is part of a bicycle:

> *He had both feet off the pedals.*

To *peddle* means to put forward or sell:

> *He peddled his ideas to the highest bidder.*

pore, pour

To *pore* means to examine closely:

> *She pored over the book, trying to find a mistake.*

If you *pour* a liquid, you cause it to flow out:

> *He poured the wine into her glass.*

practicable, practical

If something is *practicable*, it can be done:

> *Running the pipe through the wall wasn't practicable: there just wasn't enough room.*

If something is *practical*, it is useful or handy:

> *He's a very practical person and is great at making furniture.*

practice, practise

Practice is the noun, *practise* is the verb:

> *We went to football practice.*
>
> *The doctors' practice was closed.*
>
> *We will practise the presentation together tomorrow.*
>
> *She had practised her keyboard skills every night.*

prevaricate, procrastinate

Both words have something to do with hiding the truth, but there is a difference. To *prevaricate* means to hide the truth by avoiding answering a question, or by lying:

> *He prevaricated because he knew he was in the wrong.*

To *procrastinate* means to delay by wasting time:

> *He procrastinated because he was scared to start.*

principal, principle

Principal means 'main or most important'. It can also mean a headteacher or the leader of a team:

> *The principal consultant led the meeting.*

> *Equality and fairness were the principal considerations.*

A *principle* is a rule, guideline or scientific law:

> *He always followed his principles.*

> *The basic principle is that no two machines work in the same way.*

precede, proceed

To *precede* means to go before:

> *I preceded him in the management hierarchy.*

To *proceed* means to progress or continue:

> *He proceeded to talk despite the need for quiet.*

program, programme

The spelling *program* only applies to computer software; *programme* should be used in all other instances:

> *The latest version of the program was downloaded from the Internet.*

> *The training programme ensured they would continue their personal development.*

sequester, sequestrate

If something is *sequestered*, it is isolated or secluded:

> *He was sequestered from the rest of the team.*

To *sequestrate* means to confiscate:

> *The company's funds were sequestrated by the receivers.*

stationary, stationery

If something is *stationary*, it is still or motionless:

The traffic was stationary: the road was flooded.

Stationery is paper, envelopes, etc:

> *We order stationery online – it is so much more economical.*

while, whilst

Either of these words is acceptable. In the interests of clear English, however, use *while*: it sounds more modern and less pretentious than *whilst*.

who, whom

In simple terms, *who* is used for the subject of the sentence and *whom* is used for the object. An easy way of working out which is correct is to turn the sentence around and replace *who* or *whom* with *he*, *she*, *they*, *him*, *her* or *them*. *Who* should correspond with *he*, *she* or *they*; *whom* should correspond with *him*, *her* or *them*.

If you aren't sure whether to write *Who did you see?* or *Whom did you see?*, turn the sentence around. You will see that *Did you see him?* is correct rather than *Did you see he?* And *whom* corresponds to *him*:

✗ *Who did you see?*

✔ *Whom did you see?*

who, which, that

When should you use *which* and when should you use *that*? Look at the following example:

> *We stayed at the hotel which/that he recommended to us.*

This is a sentence which contains what is known as an 'identifying', 'defining' or 'restrictive' clause. Without the clause (in this case *which/that he recommended to us*) we would not know which hotel was involved.

COMMON MISTAKES

In these clauses, which we will call 'Type 1', it is perfectly acceptable to use either *which* or *that*.

However, if the sentence involves a person, then *who* is used:

✔ *We listened to the guide who was with us that day: he was much clearer than the previous one.*

✘ *We listened to the guide that was with us that day: he was much clearer than the previous one.*

Now look at the following sentence:

We stayed at The Grand Hotel, which he recommended to us.

This is a sentence which contains what is known as a 'non-identifying', 'non-defining' or 'non-restrictive' clause. This type of clause gives extra information which is not crucial to the sense of the sentence.

In these clauses, which we will call 'Type 2', you only use *which* or *who* and never *that*.

This table summarizes the differences between 'Type 1' and 'Type 2' clauses:

For Type 1 clauses	For Type 2 clauses
You do not use commas.	You normally use commas.
You <u>can</u> use *that* but *who/which* is allowed.	You <u>cannot</u> use *that*.
You can sometimes leave out *that/who/which*.	You cannot leave out *who* or *which*.

Practice exercise

These problems will test your knowledge of using the right word at the right time. In each case, choose the right word from the options given. Check your answers on pages 187–8.

1 *How does this affect/effect you?*
2 *There were adverse/averse trading conditions which affected/effected our profit.*
3 *He alluded/eluded to her in his speech but I can assure/ensure/insure you it was accidental.*
4 *The manager was responsible for appraising/apprising the team based on the number of successful sales calls each month.*
5 *He set a trap with the wallet as bait/bate and watched with baited/bated breath.*
6 *It was not a pretty cite/sight/site: compared to/with the last visit, it had changed out of all recognition.*
7 *He complemented/complimented me on my delivery style, but I wasn't complacent/complaisant: he would expect more next time.*
8 *She talked continually/continuously, which meant we couldn't hear the performance.*
9 *We've been asked to copyright/copywrite the leaflet: it needs to complement/compliment the website.*
10 *His council/counsel was different from/to/than the previous advice we had received.*
11 *The building was decimated/destroyed by the fire.*
12 *There were three criteria/criterion: weight, size and height.*
13 *She went to the meeting, despite/in spite of her misgivings.*
14 *She is so effective/efficient: everything is always delivered on time.*
15 *He was disinterested/uninterested and made the perfect referee.*
16 *The report elicited/illicited a swift response.*
17 *The desk was discreet/discrete from the table – at least four meters/metres away.*
18 *They defused/diffused the situation by announcing it was time for lunch.*
19 *The decision was eminent/immanent/imminent: then we would be entering the next faze/phase.*

COMMON MISTAKES

20 They refused to listen to any *farther/further* demands.

21 We had no cause to worry: the material was *flammable/ inflammable/non-flammable*.

22 They summarized the report verbally for the marketing director and *I/me*.

23 He *flaunted/flouted* his credentials but he wasn't offered the job.

24 I was late so I had to *forego/forgo* the first session.

25 There was a secret *hoard/horde* of stationery in the cabinet.

26 The factory needed *fewer/less* wool than before and produced *fewer/less* jumpers.

27 The garage was *licenced/licensed* by the DVLA.

28 We had *lead/led* the market but we could *loose/lose* our position unless we increase productivity.

29 None of the interviewees *was/were* suitable for the job.

30 The new production line will *militate/mitigate* the impact of shorter working hours.

31 We needed to be *practicable/practical*: it just wasn't *practicable/ practical* to get there and back in two hours.

32 They were *passed/past* caring.

33 The council *meeted/meted* out fines to all transgressors.

34 It was common *practice/practise* to leave early on a Friday.

35 We could see he was *prevaricating/procrastinating* because he simply wasn't ready.

36 We followed all the *principals/principles* we had been taught by our parents.

37 The client told us to end the contract, *that/which* was a bit of a blow.

38 When I arrive, *who/whom* should I contact?

39 I had run out of *stationary/stationery*, so I rang the supplier.

40 The money we'd set aside for tax was *sequestered/sequestrated* by the officials.

Quiz

Read these sentences and make any necessary changes. The answers are on pages 188–9.

This quiz will test the basic rules of language that are covered in Part One of this book. If you aren't sure about any of the points it covers, go back and reread the relevant section.

1   *They felt that they had one and, only one, chance to succeed.*
2   *The company was astonished at the quality but still stuck to it's decision.*
3   *In 12 year's time they will reach their maximum.*
4   *There are a number of items that you will need to bring paper with complimentary envelopes pens preferably red black and blue CD's staplers and paper clips.*
5   *Its time to take the decision as to whether you are going to make an addition to the team.*
6   *She handed it to Gavin and I: the affect was immediate.*
7   *She was so impressed with my writing that she compared it with Shakespeares!*
8   *Only ten people applied for the job, which was far less than she expected.*
9   *The pharmacy lost it's license: the reason was because of lack of organization.*
10 *Annie forgot her PIN number. When she went to the ATM.*
11 *The governments' new policy had farther impact on the price of PC's.*
12 *In the 1990's, the companies' managing director was appointed for three years service.*
13 *There was only one word for it; really terrible!*
14 *Whilst he was out of the room, the team enquired about the future prospects for the organization.*
15 *The general consensus was that the brochure was quite perfect.*

    But it would have to be replaced in six month's time.

16 The childrens' teacher would not divulge anything on principal.

17 Trefoil was determined not to loose the contract, but they were faced with a bleak outlook for future prospects.

18 In the morning as soon as Im awake I put my phone on: its part of the job.

19 None of the team want to go. Although it would have been fun.

20 Sayed was satisfied the delegates had listened learnt and worked hard now they were really going to think about their use of the English language.

Part Two

Everyday
Communication

EVERYDAY COMMUNICATION

Now that the basics are in place, it's time to turn to those everyday written communications which you will be required to produce throughout your working life. From the shortest piece of work such as a fax or memo through to full reports or sales proposals, these documents can be vital in achieving business success for your organization – and success in your career.

Why a letter?

In today's business world, letters are fast being replaced by e-mails as the primary form of written contact. But the letter still remains a crucial element of business communications: indeed, for some people and some purposes it remains the preferred choice. And its increasing rarity makes it all the more important, as it has more impact on the recipient.

A business letter offers many advantages:

- It looks so much more professional than an e-mail, particularly when it is on headed stationery and therefore communicates the organization's brand clearly and correctly.

- It will look the same when the recipient reads it as it does when the writer sends it. E-mails can look different according to the software used by the sender and recipient and thus can sometimes create an unprofessional impression.

- It can be easily photocopied or filed.

- The sender's signature gives it a more personal feel and therefore greater impact.

- There is something psychologically different about opening an envelope and discovering a letter, rather than just receiving an e-mail at your computer screen: it has more 'gravitas'.

Of course, e-mails are more immediate – but this can sometimes be their downfall. All too often e-mails are written and sent too quickly and receive unconsidered responses. Letters are less immediate: this gives you the opportunity to consider and review the content more carefully.

LETTERS

Before you start

Before embarking on a letter, it's important to plan it. Ask the following questions and keep them in mind when you start to write:

- Why am I writing this letter? Am I communicating new information, introducing myself, following up a conversation, replying to something, selling something, using it to accompany something I've enclosed, or giving instructions?

- Who is the recipient? How well do I know them? What is their knowledge of the subject? How much do they already know and how much more do they need to know? How familiar are they with the subject matter or the terminology?

- What do I need to say? How much do I have to explain? What is the main point of the letter? What details are needed?

- How am I writing? Is it a formal document or is it less formal and more conversational?

- What is the desired outcome? What do I want the recipient to do? Does my letter require a reply, will it be followed up by a telephone call, or will it mark the end of the communication?

The structure of business letters

There was a time when letters varied considerably in style, but now there is something approaching consensus on how they should be set out. The most common style – and the one that probably looks the most professional – is what is known as the blocked style. This involves no indenting at the beginning of paragraphs, with all text starting at the same point on the left hand side of the page. It also removes all punctuation in the date, address, greeting and farewell. The style was originally introduced in the days of manual typewriters, where eliminating indenting and some punctuation would save someone in the typing pool a considerable amount of time and therefore increase productivity. But, in fact, it also looks good.

The letter below shows an example of the blocked style.

Suits for You
54 High Street
Bristol
BS1 4ZZ

14 November 2007
Ref: AC/504/BB

John Smith
Managing Director
Busby Shirts Ltd
Busby House
Walton Street
London
EC1V 4VW

Dear Mr Smith

Order for cotton shirts

Following our telephone conversation this morning, I would like to confirm my order for 36 cotton shirts.

As discussed, we will display these in a prominent position in our shop window. We will also promote them to our customers through our regular newsletter.

I would like to take this opportunity to thank you for your support and I look forward to continuing our joint venture.

Yours sincerely

Frederick Jones
Managing Director

LETTERS

Note these points about the layout of the letter on page 83:

* In this instance the date comes first. The position of the date may vary according to house style and is sometimes placed after the address. The important point is to be consistent across the entire organization.

* The style used here for giving the date is perhaps the most common style for business correspondence, but there are others, as noted below. Again, consistency is key.

* References are still used by some organizations as they help the retrieval of information from files. The reference comes in this instance under the date. Sometimes it may be used as a heading after the greeting.

* The address is blocked left with no punctuation used.

* It is quite acceptable these days to give the name above the address without a title (ie John Smith or Mary Jones, rather than Mr Smith or Dr Jones). Your company's house style may dictate that you use a title. Again, consistency is key.

* The greeting stands to the left with no punctuation. (See page 85 for guidance on correct greetings.)

* A heading is very useful in stating clearly what the letter is about, although it is not always needed.

* The main body of the text is blocked left, with no indenting, single spacing, and a double space between paragraphs.

* The ending is blocked left with no punctuation. (See pages 85–6 for guidance on correct endings.)

* The sender's name and role is blocked left, with no punctuation.

Dates

The most common format for writing dates in business correspondence is *14 November 2007*. Other acceptable formats are *14th November 2007*, *November 14 2007* or *November 14th 2007*. As always, the most important thing is to be consistent in the style you use.

Addresses

The accepted format is to have one line for each separate element:

> *Mr D Smith*
> *Managing Director*
> *Smith & Co Ltd*
> *Smith House*
> *Smith Street*
> *London*
> *EC1 2DD*

Greetings

Follow these guidelines when addressing the person you are writing to:

* Always use *Dear*.
* If possible, address the recipient by name rather than using *Sir/Madam*.
* First names are much more commonly used in business today, but be sure it is appropriate before using this style.
* If you don't know the recipient's name, then address them by *Dear Sir* or *Dear Madam*. If you don't know the gender of the recipient then use *Dear Sir/Madam*.
* Do not use any punctuation.

Farewells

* Business letters usually end with either *Yours sincerely* or *Yours faithfully*.
* There are strict rules on which one you use (see the table on the next page). To summarize, if you are addressing *Dear Sir/Madam*, you always end with *Yours faithfully*; if you are using a name in the greeting, you never use *Yours faithfully*.
* If the recipient is well known to you, you can use a more informal ending such as *With best regards* (see the table on the next page).
* Do not use any punctuation.

LETTERS

Situation	Greeting	Ending
You don't know the name of the recipient of your letter	Dear Sir Dear Madam Dear Sir/Madam	Yours faithfully
You know the name of the recipient of your letter	Dear Mr Smith Dear Mrs Jones Dear Mrs Davis Dear Dr Williams	Yours sincerely
You know the person well and don't wish to be formal	Dear Andrea Dear Colin	With best wishes With best regards Kindest regards All the best

Content

A business letter should always be:

- **Clear**: It should say exactly what you want to say and leave no doubt as to its purpose and the next step. Follow the rules about clear English explained in Part One.
- **Complete**: It should fully explain what the letter is about and not leave any unanswered questions.
- **Concise**: It should say what it needs to say once and only say what is necessary.
- **Correct**: It should be *factually* correct; it should have the correct *tone* for the subject matter and the recipient; and all grammar, spelling and punctuation should be correct.
- **Courteous**: Never insult, even if you are complaining. Always keep it polite.
- **Careful**: Never threaten, never overstate. Make sure you can justify what you say.
- **Considered**: After you've written the letter, consider it carefully. Think about how the recipient will interpret it. Does it say everything that's needed? Does it explain everything clearly?

Think of these as the 'seven Cs' of business letters.

Structuring the information

It makes it easier to construct a letter if you think of it in three sections.

The **introduction** should state up front why you are writing. This section is often just a single paragraph, or perhaps even a single sentence. It will acknowledge any previous communication (for example, a letter, an e-mail, a meeting or a telephone conversation).

The **main body** will then develop the letter and deal with the subject in detail. It may be several paragraphs. It's fine to use bullet points to get over several points: what's important is that it gets over the information, following the seven Cs.

The **ending** will restate the purpose (using phrases such as *Once again, thank you for your interest*) and summarize the next step or call to action. It will also sign off in a standard way to bring the letter to an end. Often it will use a phrase such as *I look forward to hearing from you*.

Example

The letter on page 88 has this structure, with bullets used to make a list of points. Notice how it follows the seven Cs, and in particular how it remains courteous despite the content.

Jolly Good Restaurant
7 The Parade
Manchester
M2 6MM

19 November 2007

Peter Harris
1 The Square
Manchester
M1 4DD

Dear Mr Harris

Thank you for your letter. I am very sorry you were not satisfied with the service you received at our restaurant. I would however make the following points:

- You had booked a table for 8pm and arrived at 8.50pm. We carefully stagger our bookings to ensure we can give the maximum attention to each of our guests. Unfortunately your late arrival disrupted our careful planning for the evening.
- Your booking was for four people but your party comprised six. We did our very best to accommodate you but inevitably there was some pressure on space.
- We do not claim to be a family restaurant and therefore your request for children's portions was not possible.

We do however accept that the service you received was not up to our normal standards, and we would like to make this up to you in some way. We would therefore like to offer you a free bottle of house wine to accompany your meal if you visit our restaurant on another occasion.

Yours sincerely

Peter Chef

Practice exercise

Look at the letter below and rewrite to ensure it has the appropriate style, structure and format. Compare your version with the one on page 190.

The IT Centre
50 Oxford Street
Bournemouth
BH1 9AA

19th November, 2007

Mr. P. Smith,
1 The avenue,
New Malden
Surrey
K.T.3 1BB

Dear Mr P Smith

Please find herewith for your convenience 30 ink cartridges. Let me know you have received them. This is what you asked for when we talked on the phone today. As I mentioned, they are the last we have in stock but we may get some more soon. I think you'd like to have more when they arrive.

Yours faithfully

Mr Jones
Warehouse Manager

LETTERS

Checklist

- Plan your letter and be clear what you want to achieve before you start writing.
- Set your letter out according to the standard format.
- Take care to use the appropriate greeting and farewell.
- Your letter should follow the seven Cs of business letters: clear, complete, concise, correct, courteous, careful and considered.

E-mails

E-mails are rapidly becoming the main form of communication in business and in many instances are replacing other forms of written and verbal communication.

It's all too easy to make mistakes with e-mail messages. The key is to regard them as electronic letters and to pay them as much attention as you would a standard business letter. All the same rules apply, especially the seven Cs of letter writing (see pages 86–7). Perhaps the most important of these as far as e-mail is concerned, however, is 'consider': think long and hard about it before you press that 'Send' button.

Because of its instant nature, many people just rush off a response and send it without thought. And because it feels informal, less care is taken over its content – and particularly how the recipient will read it. It often has a conversational tone, and that tone can be misinterpreted by the recipient.

So the basic rule is: take care and make sure you say exactly what you mean. If possible, write the e-mail, put it into your 'Drafts' section and read it again later before you send it.

Rules for writing e-mail

As the use of e-mail has spread, it has acquired its own system of rules (sometimes humorously referred to as 'netiquette'):

- Remember that e-mails are easily forwarded to other people, with the e-mail trail visible through the body of the message. So you can never guarantee who will read it. Never, ever, put anything in an e-mail which you wouldn't say to someone's face.

- Don't rush your response to an e-mail. Write it, leave it and come back to it. Read it again before you send it.

- Think about the possible interpretations of your words. You may be thinking it in one tone but the reader may 'hear' it in another. Could it be misconstrued?

- If you are copying in other people, think about the implications. Copying in someone's boss can make it seem threatening; copying in colleagues or subordinates could undermine the recipient's position.

- Avoid writing IN CAPITAL LETTERS. It makes it sound as if you are shouting. It also looks very odd and unprofessional.

- Avoid the temptation to use too many exclamation marks or ellipses (running dots after words…). It lessens the impact and looks unprofessional.

- Use emoticons (those little pictures created by a combination of keyboard characters) with care. They can really annoy some people. Try to say what you mean through the words you use.

- Avoid using too many abbreviations and acronyms (see the table on pages 96–7). Some people will not understand them. Only use them with people you know well.

- Remember that anyone copied in on the e-mail can see a list of all recipients – and therefore see their e-mail addresses. This may be regarded as an intrusion of privacy. Use the blind copy function instead (bcc). If you are sending to a group of people who do not know each other, send to all as blind copies and put yourself as the recipient.

Before you write

There are several things to consider before you start to compose the actual message. Firstly, make sure the address is correct, otherwise it will not reach the intended recipient. Most companies have their own format (often firstname@xyz.co.uk or firstname.surname@xyz.co.uk). Never guess: always check. Addresses are normally in lower case (although this is not crucial for successful transmission).

You should also use the subject line to summarize the content. Many users receive large numbers of spam e-mails, so if the subject means nothing to the recipient you risk it being deleted before it is even read.

Greetings and farewells

Avoid the ubiquitous *Hi* to open an e-mail unless it is to someone you know very well and you are sure they will not be offended by it. It is perfectly acceptable to write *Dear Sajid* or even just *Sajid*.

If you are e-mailing someone you know by name only, then *Yours sincerely* is a perfectly acceptable way to end, although it is rarely used. If you are writing to someone you have communicated with before, then use *Regards*, *Best regards*, *Kindest regards* or something similar.

Most organizations lay down a standard format for an e-mail signature. This should include your full name, position in the company, address and telephone numbers. It may also include other general company information, such as fax number, website, and a company marketing statement. It's also a company decision whether this is appended to replies to e-mails received as well as new e-mails. But don't just use the formal signature for sign off: it is too impersonal. Put your name before it: just your first name if appropriate, otherwise use your first name and surname.

The message itself

Consider the structure in the same way as a letter (see page 87). Think of it in three sections: an introduction, a main body and an ending.

Example

There is an example of a well-constructed e-mail on page 94.

```
To: steve@genericcampaigns.com
From: sam@lighthouse.co.uk
Subject: Marketing Proposal
Attachment: Generic Campaigns Marketing Proposal
October 2008

Steve:

As promised, I attach our Marketing Proposal for the
organic cheese project.

We've taken on board all the points raised at our
last meeting and have incorporated them in section
3. We have also added key messages and profiles of
our team.

If there's anything else you need, then please let
me know.

With best regards.

Sam

                                    Sam Watson
                        Lighthouse Communications
             7 Romsey Street, Southampton SO1 2BB
                               Tel: 023 765 4233
                            Mobile: 07000 123456
                            www.lighthousecomms.org
                            Lighting up your marketing.
```

Tone

E-mails tend to be fairly informal in style, but this is not an excuse
for sloppy writing nor for lack of clarity. If in doubt, adopt a formal
style. Here are a few guidelines:

- If the e-mail is going to a recipient outside your organization, apply the same rules as you would for a letter. The style should be formal.

* If the e-mail is internal (ie going to a work colleague) you can be less formal but still be careful: you don't want to get a reputation for sloppiness.

* If you are replying to an e-mail, adopt a similar tone to the original.

* Remember that your e-mail can easily be forwarded to other people: be careful what you say.

Attachments

E-mails are often used to send documents to recipients. Here are a few guidelines to consider:

* Think about the title of the document you have attached. Don't make it too generic: it may not mean anything to the recipient or it may get lost among several documents with the same name. Be specific: give it a title which has a good chance of being unique and meaningful to the recipient.

* Make sure the attachment you are sending is the right document and the most recent version. It's a useful check to attach a document and then open it via the e-mail before you send it (remembering to close it again). This way you can be certain it is precisely the document you intended, in the right version.

* Be careful attaching very large documents: some recipients have a limited in-box capacity which may not be able to cope with them.

* Always check that the recipient has the appropriate software to open the attachment.

Abbreviations

It is customary to use many abbreviations in informal e-mail. These often take the form of a common expression being represented only by the initial letters of the words. Many of these are now used routinely, although it is a good idea to make sure those people to whom you send messages are familiar with these before you start to include them in your messages.

E-MAILS

Here are some of the more common abbreviations encountered in e-mail:

Abbreviation	Meaning
AFAIK	as far as I know
AFK	away from keyboard
ASAP	as soon as possible
ATB	all the best
B4	before
BAK	back at keyboard
BBL	be back later
BTDT	been there done that
BTW	by the way
CLD	could
CUL8R	see you later
F2F	face to face
FAQ	frequently asked question
FYI	for your information
GAL	get a life
GTG	got to go
HTH	hope this helps
IMHO	in my humble opinion
IMO	in my opinion
IOW	in other words
L8	late
L8R	later
LOL	laughing out loud (when someone has written something funny)
MSG	message
MYOB	mind your own business
NE1	anyone
NRN	no reply necessary
NW!	no way!

OMG	Oh my God!
OTOH	on the other hand
PLS	please
POV	point of view
TBD	to be discussed
THRU	through
TIA	thanks in advance
TNX	thanks
TTYL	talk to you later
TVM	thanks very much
WRT	with regard to
XOXOXO	hugs and kisses

Practice exercise

Here is the body of an e-mail from a supplier to a new customer. The e-mail is to Barbara Bathson and is from Nigel Marr, who is Senior Sales Consultant at lighting supplier Bright Lights Ltd. Today's date is 8th November 2007. Add in a subject line and rewrite it to the correct format, style and tone. Compare your version with the one on page 191.

Hi.

Got your order yesterday – 7 Macintosh glass lampholders and three pull switches. Should be despatched tomorrow but can't be sure. Will let you know, when I find out, when you will receive them. BTW the seventh lampholder will be free because of a special offer we've got on at the moment.

We're really pleased to have got your order and to be supplying you with this ☺

Cheers.

Nigel

Checklist

- Pay as much care and consideration to writing an e-mail as you would when writing a letter.
- Observe the conventional 'netiquette' of e-mail users.
- Just because e-mails can be informal, that is not an excuse for sloppy writing or lack of clarity.
- Remember that e-mails can easily be copied to other people; be careful what you say.

Faxes and memos

Faxes

Fax is a short form of *facsimile*. Faxes are used less frequently since the advent of e-mail, but they still have a role to play in business. They are particularly useful as a way of sending urgent information which cannot be sent by e-mail (eg copies of documents, or to confirm orders speedily on headed paper).

Here is an example of how a fax might be written:

> Computer Resources
> 15 Way Road
> Watford
> WD1 1AS
>
> **FAX**
> To: Fred Hughes   From: Peter Jones
> Fax: 0112 34567   Date: 1st January 2007
> Tel: 0112 34566 No. of pages: 4
> Re: 2007 Catalogue
>
> ---
>
> Fred:
>
> Attached are the three pages we discussed, with corrections marked. Please let me know if you have difficulty reading them.
>
> We'll expect the next version on Monday morning.
>
> Thanks.
>
> Peter

FAXES AND MEMOS

If you need to send information by fax, follow these general guidelines:

- Faxes must always have a cover sheet, which includes details of the sender (name, contact numbers), date, number of pages transmitted, recipient and subject.
- The style can be concise but is usually formal.
- It is not always necessary to include a formal greeting or ending.
- Faxes can be signed by hand, unless produced automatically by computer.

Memos

Memos are an even more endangered species than faxes: they have been almost entirely replaced by e-mails. They are still used in some organizations however as a means of communicating among colleagues.

Memos are similar in format to faxes and should contain:

- details of the originator including name, department, extension number and e-mail address
- the recipient's name and department or group name
- a list of those copied in on the memo (indicated by 'Cc')
- the date
- the subject

The body copy of a memo should be formal in tone and as concise as possible, but there is no need for a greeting or formal farewell.

The structure should follow the same order as a letter: there should be an introduction which explains the purpose of the memo, followed by the main body which lays out the detail, and an ending which summarizes the next step or the required outcome.

The general rule for memos is that they should be as concise as possible: one page is fine; two pages is the maximum.

Example

There is an example below of how a memo might be written.

Memo

To: Marketing Department
From: Sally Smith, Personnel (sally@reallybiggroup.com); ext 234
Cc: Personnel Department
Date: 1st November 2007

Subject: Christmas party

We've been asked to organize this year's party and would welcome input from Marketing.

We have a number of questions and would appreciate your thoughts:

- Should we hold the party at lunchtime or in the evening?
- Should partners be invited?
- What format should it take: a meal, a disco or simply drinks and snacks?
- Should we hold it as normal in the convention centre or is there another suitable venue?

We'd be grateful for your input by the end of the week.

Many thanks.

Checklist

- Both faxes and memos should be concise and formal.
- Include details of sender and recipient(s) as well as date and subject on a cover sheet (for a fax) or the header (for a memo).

Materials for meetings

Agendas

A well-run meeting depends as much on a well-planned agenda as it does on a firm and decisive Chair. Taking some time before a meeting to think about what needs to be discussed and in what order can make all the difference.

An agenda should be brief and to the point; it should contain a basic list of the things to be discussed and in the order they should be discussed. Copies are normally sent to attendees prior to the meeting, so they can prepare as necessary.

Agendas may contain the following, but not all elements are always needed:

- title of the meeting or reason for the meeting
- date, time and location
- a list of those required to attend, usually in alphabetical order but with officers first
- appointment of Chair (this will not be necessary if there is already a Chair in place)
- apologies for absence (these may be sent in advance or presented at the meeting)
- minutes of the last meeting: an opportunity to review the previous minutes, correct any errors and give formal approval
- matters arising: an opportunity for attendees to comment on anything which is relevant to items discussed at the last meeting
- correspondence received: any letters, e-mails, etc which should be brought to the members' attention
- reports from officers: an opportunity for the Chair, Secretary and other officials to bring members up to date on their activities

- specific subjects for discussion: items which have to be raised at the meeting and are known about in advance
- any other business (AOB): new items not known about in advance and raised by members
- next meeting: agreeing the date, time and venue

Example

The layout of an agenda should be clear and concise, as in the example below.

Arts Foundation Committee Meeting
28th November 2007
7.30pm, Loxborne Village Hall

Attendees: Anne Witheney (Chair), Paul Booth (Treasurer), Harriet Cases (Secretary), Isabelle Marcel, Simon Kidd, Carl Badgen, Michael Tamplin, Shelagh Wright.

1. Apologies
2. Minutes of last meeting: held 26th September 2007
3. Correspondence
4. Chair's Report
5. Treasurer's Report
6. Items for discussion
    6.1. Somerset Awards for All grant application
    6.2. Festival of Song
    6.3. Art in the Community project
    6.4. Logo and new stationery
7. AOB
8. Date and venue for next meeting

Minutes of a meeting

Minutes are a formal record of a meeting. Their aim is not to report everything that was discussed, but simply to give a very brief summary. Their most important function is to record any decisions taken, and specifically what actions should be taken and by whom.

MATERIALS FOR MEETINGS

They should provide a useful reminder of what took place to those attending, as well as summarizing clearly for those unable to attend.

Here are a few guidelines:

* Minutes should follow the pattern of the relevant agenda, so the structure will already be in place.
* Adopt a formal tone: minutes should be impersonal, generally written in the passive voice (see pages 11–12); they should use indirect speech rather than reporting the actual words spoken.
* Sentences should be short and concise.
* Bullet points are a useful tool for displaying simple lists.
* Any decisions taken should be clearly noted; if votes are taken these should be recorded clearly.
* Action points should be noted: these should record the subject and person to carry out the action.
* There should be a clear numbering system to make it easy to refer to specific points in future documents.

Minutes would normally include the following items:

* a title with the name of the committee or nature of the meeting
* the date of the meeting, the location and the time the meeting started
* those attending (usually listed alphabetically but with the officers first)
* apologies for absence
* any corrections to the minutes of the previous meeting plus formal approval
* matters arising: notes of any updates to items discussed at the previous meeting
* officers' reports: notes of any reports made by the Chair, Treasurer, Secretary or any other officer
* items for discussion: items included on the agenda, with a brief summary of discussions and any action points

**Arts Foundation Committee Meeting
28th November 2007
7.30pm, Loxborne Village Hall**

Attendees: Anne Witheney (Chair), Paul Booth (Treasurer), Harriet Cases (Secretary), Isabelle Marcel, Simon Kidd, Carl Badgen.

1. Apologies: Michael Tamplin, Shelagh Wright.

2. Minutes of last meeting: held 26th September 2007. The total funds in the current account were £456 not £465. With this correction, the Minutes were approved and signed.

3. Matters arising: none.

4. Correspondence:
4.1. A letter had been received from Lord Axbridge, enclosing a cheque for £50 to support the Foundation's activities. It was agreed that the Secretary would write a letter of thanks. **Action: HC.**
4.2. A letter had been received from Mrs Tillgood, thanking the Committee for its donation to the school.
4.3. An e-mail had been received from Loxborne District Council (LDC), with details of all arts events during 2008. This included The Festival of Song.

5. Chair's Report:
5.1. The Chair had attended the LDC quarterly meeting: this was very poorly attended and no decisions were made.
5.2. The Chair had discussed using the Loxborne Village Hall for meetings with the Chair of the Parish Council: this can continue until the end of 2008.

6. Treasurer's Report: There was no change to the financial position.

7. Items for discussion:
7.1. Somerset Awards for All grant application: no news had been received from Somerset CC. The Secretary agreed to chase. **Action: HC.**
7.2. Festival of Song:
• Three more choirs had agreed to participate: Steam, Gravel Heat and Midsummer Madness.
• Mrs Smith had agreed to the use of her garden.
• Steve Rayman was now designing the posters and would deliver the artwork by the end of December.
7.3. Art in the Community: following a discussion, a vote was taken and it was unanimously agreed to postpone the event until Autumn 2008.
7.4. Logo and new stationery: no progress had been made. The Secretary agreed to ask Steve Rayman to quote for this project. **Action: HC.**

8. AOB:
8.1. IM asked if members could let her know their preferences for the Christmas dinner by e-mail by 15th December. **Action: All.**
8.2. CB reminded members that he would present his paper on Community Art on 3rd January at Axbridge Town Hall, 7.30pm. Tickets are still available.
8.3. It was agreed that in future minutes would be circulated electronically rather than by post. Members should send their e-mail addresses to the Secretary at AFC@bt.com. **Action: All.**

9. Date and venue for next meeting:
Friday 27th January, 7.30pm, Ashford Village Hall.

The meeting closed at 8.45pm.

MATERIALS FOR MEETINGS

- any other business: items raised at the meeting including names of the person raising them, a brief summary of the ensuing discussion and action points
- date, time and place of the next meeting
- time the meeting closed

Example
On page 105 there is a good example of a set of minutes, relating to the meeting whose agenda was outlined on page 103.

Contact reports
A contact report is simply the name given to minutes taken at a business meeting between two or more different organizations: they are likely to be meeting to discuss a project or contract.

Here are a few things to remember if you have to compile this sort of report:

- The main reason for a contact report is to record decisions and actions.
- It is a less formal record than a set of minutes.
- There are unlikely to be apologies.
- There are no officers' reports.
- There will be no votes but rather agreed actions.

Example
There is a typical example of a contact report on page 107.

Contact Report

Client: TechnoForm
Date of meeting: 30th November 2007
Subject: PR Review
Attendees: Chris Rigby, Graham Brown (TechnoForm); Sally Thomas, Peter Thwaite (Good to Talk).

Website: Good to Talk had now reviewed and rewritten five pages of the TechnoForm website. These were approved and likely to go live next week.

Brochure: Some changes are needed to the layout of the back page to incorporate the overseas addresses. Good to Talk will arrange this with the designer and resubmit the design. **Action: GTT/ST.**

Features:
- The IT Talking article is now placed in Good Business magazine and should appear in February.
- The Broadband Narrowband article is with TechnoForm for approval and should be ready for the deadline of 3rd December. **Action: TF/GB.**
- Good to Talk will now prepare the press release on the Science Park contract and will submit to TF for approval. **Action: GTT/ PT.**

Media Training: This will take place on 6th January at the TechnoForm offices. Good to Talk will submit a pre-course questionnaire by the end of December. **Action: GTT/ST.**

Evaluation: The Evaluation Report will be ready for review by the end of January. This will include all coverage plus the advertising value equivalent. A full breakdown of likely coverage between January and March 2008 is also required. **Action: GTT/ST.**

Next meeting: to be arranged.

MATERIALS FOR MEETINGS

Checklist

- An agenda should contain a basic list of the things to be discussed and in the order they should be discussed.

- Minutes give a brief summary of what was discussed and any decisions taken.

- Minutes should be impersonal, using the passive voice and indirect speech.

- Both agendas and minutes should be clearly numbered.

Reports

What is a report?

A report is a formal document which is produced as the result of an investigation or research. It will often contain a considerable amount of information and therefore it will be far clearer and communicate more effectively if it is structured in easy-to-digest sections. The emphasis must be on logical presentation and ease of reference.

Before starting a report, you need to identify the following:

- **Purpose**: Why am I writing this? Is it to propose a change, review something that's already happened, report an incident, summarize a weightier matter, evaluate something, propose something new, explain a procedure or illuminate a problem?
- **Objective**: What is the desired outcome? What should the audience be left with? Should it inform, describe, explain, instruct, evaluate, recommend, provoke or persuade (or is it all these things)?
- **Audience**: Who will read it? How familiar are they with reports? How much time do they have to absorb it? How familiar are they with the subject matter; how much do they already know; how much more do they need to know? What is their attitude to the subject and what is their attitude to me? What is their level of understanding?
- **Resources**: How much time do I have? What is my budget for preparing it? What can I use?
- **Information**: What research do I need to undertake? How much information is already available? What needs to be included and what can be discarded?

Structure of a report

The structure of a report will vary according to its content and length, but in essence it will always follow a similar pattern. Not all elements will always be necessary, but this list offers a good starting point:

* title page
* contents
* summary
* terms of reference
* methods of investigation
* findings
* conclusions
* recommendations
* appendices
* bibliography
* index

Let's now look at each section in more detail.

Title page
This should contain the following elements:

* the title of the report (it's often useful to have a main heading and a more explanatory subheading)
* the author, including name and role
* date
* other relevant information: this might include the author's company/organization, level of confidentiality, a reference number, and any copyright information

Contents page
This should comprise a complete list of the contents of the report, with section numbers and page numbers. Its purpose is to make it easy to dip into different sections as required. Remember that, if you change the content of the report at any time after you have created the contents page, this may have implications for page numbers.

As a rough rule of thumb, any report over four pages requires a contents page.

Summary

A summary is only necessary if you have produced a long report and need a snapshot of its contents. The point of this section is to state briefly the key points: the purpose, the main findings, the main conclusions and main recommendations. Although it comes third in the report, it will be one of the last things to be written. When writing it, think which parts are the most important and what really needs to be communicated to the reader. There is more detailed advice about how to summarize information on pages 164–5.

Terms of reference

This section lays out the ground rules: what the report is about; what you were asked to produce and by whom; whether that is what you have actually produced and whether you have also looked at other matters.

Methods of investigation

This section explains the procedure you have used to produce the report. It should cover how you gathered the information: for example, through interviews, meetings, site visits, studying reference materials or observing procedures. It should also explain how long the process took.

In a shorter report, it may be possible to combine the terms of reference and the methods of investigation into a single section and simply call it the 'introduction'.

Findings

This is the main section of the report and will set out the results of your investigations, your findings, arguments, options and ideas. It will be factual and unbiased: it is simply a statement of facts, in a logical and coherent order. This is likely to be longer than any other section of the report.

REPORTS

The most successful way to present it is by following a logical system of heading and subheadings. Some possible formats are explained on pages 113–14.

Conclusions

This should contain only the main inferences you have drawn from the findings: there should be no new material and the section should be a logical progression from what preceded it. It is not a summary.

In some reports, there may be no conclusions to be drawn from the findings. If so, there is no need to include this section.

Recommendations

This section will set out the steps you think should be taken as a result of your investigation, based logically on the conclusions you have drawn. It will be different in style, as it will use the words 'should' and 'should be' rather than 'is' and 'has been'. It's a good idea to review your terms of reference before writing your recommendations, as this will force you to think through what your remit really is.

Not all reports require a separate section for recommendations: some reports may simply be statements of facts, with no recommendations for future actions required; in other reports, it may make sense to combine the conclusions and recommendations in a single section.

Appendices

Any material which would break the main flow of the report should be put in an appendix. This applies particularly to any supporting information, such as copies of forms used for interviewing, diagrams, maps, tables or lists. Appendices should follow the order in which they are referenced in the body of the document and be labelled accordingly. It is crucial that the number or letter used to label an appendix matches the one given at the appropriate place in the main body of the report.

Bibliography

This will contain an alphabetical list of any material you have used to compile your report, including books, websites, and journal articles.

Index

An index is only needed if the report is very long. It will list key terms in alphabetical order and will have corresponding page numbers, to help readers find the places in the report where those terms are mentioned.

Numbering systems

A numbering system is not only vital in making your report easy to read; it is also a really useful way to help you plan your report. It will ensure information is presented consistently throughout, and that matters of equal importance are given equal prominence. The system will probably reflect the fact that there are different levels of information in the report.

There are many different formats for numbering paragraphs and subparagraphs in reports. The most important point is to be consistent and use a system which is easy to follow.

Here is an example of a very common format:

1.	*Summary*
2.	*Terms of Reference*
3.	*Findings*
3.1.	*External Findings*
3.1.1.	*National*
3.1.2.	*International*
3.2.	*Internal Findings*
3.2.1.	*Managers*
3.2.2.	*Support Staff*

The same information could be presented using a different numbering system:

A. *Summary*
B. *Terms of Reference*
C. *Findings*
    a) *External Findings*
        i) *National*
        ii) *International*
    b) *Internal Findings*
        i) *Managers*
        ii) *Support Staff*

When you come to label appendices, you can use either numbers or letters, but you must be consistent and stick to the same method throughout. So if you have three appendices, they will either follow the format Appendix 1, Appendix 2, Appendix 3 or else Appendix A, Appendix B, Appendix C.

Tone and language

As with any other piece of business writing, the most important aspect of a report is that it is written clearly, concisely and correctly. But it is also important to remember that a report is a formal document and must not be in any way personalized. It has to be presented in an independent and unbiased way, and the language, vocabulary and tone used must reflect this.

Some points to note:

* Never personalize a report by using phrases such as *I spoke to three people*. Instead, it is perfectly acceptable to use the passive form: *Three people were interviewed.*

* Do not record the exact words spoken (as in *She said 'I'd prefer to rent'*); use an indirect form such as *He stated that the room had been empty* or *She indicated that her preference was to rent rather than buy.*

* Avoid the temptation of using excessively complicated language. Keep it as simple as you can to avoid sounding pompous.

* Avoid technical jargon. Think about your readership's level of

knowledge and define terms they may not understand the first time you use them. You should also define any abbreviations and acronyms unless they are in common usage.

- Remember that the recommendations section requires a different grammatical form as you switch to saying what *should be* done or *may be* done.

Example
Here is an example of a report which follows all the basic rules:

To: Julie Oliver, Managing Director
From: Alexander White, Training Manager
Date: 16 September 2007
Subject: Provision of in-house training courses

1. Introduction
The purpose of this report is to examine the feasibility of holding all training courses in house. External training providers were consulted, estimates of training costs were received and comparative costs examined. Questionnaires were completed by 80 employees from four departments and 10 of the respondents were interviewed by members of the training department.

2. Advantages
2.1   Following consultation with four of the company's regularly used external training providers, it was calculated that in-house training would reduce the present cost by 26% in the first year (see Appendix A).
2.2   It was felt by 65% of the staff that training courses could be better designed to suit the specific needs of the organization, and therefore bring benefit to the company as a whole.
2.3   45% of those who responded to the questionnaire felt that they were more likely to participate in training courses if they were held on site.

3. Disadvantages
3.1   Some respondents, particularly in the sales department, expressed concern that valuable business contacts arising from external training courses would be lost if all training was held in house.

3.2 Some training needs are very specific, and may only be required by one or two staff members. It was felt that these could not always be met by in-house training courses, as the necessary expertise could not always be brought in from outside.

3.3 Participation in external training courses is seen by 30% of respondents as a perk of the job, and it was felt that this motivational factor would be diminished with the provision of all training in house.

4. Conclusions

As a result of the analysis of the advantages and disadvantages of providing all training in-house, the following conclusions can be drawn:

- Considerable savings will be made in the immediate future if in-house training courses are introduced.
- The staff response is favourable overall, particularly at higher levels of management, although in some departments the loss of external training courses is seen to be a real disadvantage, with the loss of business contacts.
- While many employees feel that in-house training is a positive move and is likely to increase participation, 30% regarded it as a loss of a perk.

5. Recommendations

- In-house training courses should be introduced where a significant number of participants are required to attend.
- Where there are fewer than five participants, external courses should be an option.
- Staff should be consulted regularly as to the level of satisfaction with in-house training courses, and feedback regarding motivational factors should be addressed.

Practice exercise

Rewrite the report on pages 117–18 to make it more professional and easier to use. Pay particular attention to the Conclusions and Recommendations and make sure they are appropriate. Compare your version with the one on pages 192–3.

ASTEROID ELECTRO MECHANICAL SYSTEMS PLC

Investigation report into health and safety hazards at the Bournemouth site

Date of submission: 25 June 2007
Compiled by: PD Smith, Safety Officer
For the attention of: GH Merryweather, Managing Director

Terms of Reference

I was asked to investigate all the health and safety hazards at the Bournemouth site which may be in contravention of the Health and Safety at Work Act.

The Managing Director asked me to do this for the possible visit by the Government Inspector some time. I've just been appointed Safety Officer and was given a deadline of end of June 2007. I was asked to make recommendations for any improvements which should be made.

METHODS OF INVESTIGATION

I used four methods:

Legislation: I looked at the Health & Safety at Work Act.

Observation: I inspected the Research and Development Annex, the Production Workshops and the office-based departments (Personnel, Finance and Marketing). I spent two hours in each location, observing and taking notes.

Interviews: I interviewed the line managers for each location to ascertain whether they had observed any problems. I also asked them how well they knew their own responsibilities under the Act.

Informal discussions: I carried these out with some employees while carrying out observations.

Findings/analysis of information

Legislation: It's clear in this that all staff could be liable under the Act were an accident to occur. Responsibilities are clarified for senior management, supervisory staff and the employees themselves. A short guide appears in the first Appendix.

Observation:
R&D Annex: The environment here is a 'clean' one and conditions are generally good. However, I noticed during my visit that one young graduate trainee was observed attempting to lift a very heavy CO_2 cylinder. When I questioned him, he said he had been told to do this by the project leader and that all personnel had to do this from time to time to maintain tests.

The workshops: In most workshops, I could not see any problems, but in Workshop C the ventilation had broken down and men were working with open coats: it was a very hot day. These could easily catch in the machinery and cause accidents.

The offices: Generally, I felt these had good working conditions. The administration office however had too many extension leads and these were trailing all over the floor. I felt there is a general carelessness over trailing leads in all offices.

Interviews:
I asked the Project Manager about the CO_2 cylinders. He said he himself had lifted them sometimes and that one trainee had suffered from a strained back. He'd asked the R&D Manager for trolleys for this but none had arrived yet.

I asked the Workshop C Supervisor about the ventilation. He said he'd sent a memo to Maintenance a week earlier which had requested action but the reply said they were too short-staffed because of holidays and would do it 'as soon as possible'. He did realize his responsibilities, which had been covered in a training course.
I interviewed two relevant office supervisors: both indicated that the extension leads were needed.

Informal discussions with employees: no one seemed to realize his possible liability under the Act, although all employees had signed contracts of employment which stated that they were responsible for their own safety.

Conclusions
We need some kind of lifting method for the CO_2 cylinders. If there is a back injury, the company will be liable.
We need more temporary staff in the maintenance department to mend the ventilation.
If this were carried out, we could fit more sockets to get rid of trailing leads.
We need to carry out training for staff on safety at all levels.

Recommendations
We should contact Industrial Lifting Gear plc to help with the lifting problem.
We should engage four temporary maintenance staff. The managing director must demand immediate attention to the ventilation in workshop C and the supply of power sockets in the Administration Office.
The Training Office must run some safety courses for all personnel. I suggest Safety forms an important part of induction days.

Checklist

- When writing a report, the emphasis should be on logical presentation and ease of reference.
- Use a consistent numbering system to help your readers.
- The tone should be impersonal, using the passive voice and indirect speech.

Sales proposals

What is a sales proposal?

A sales proposal is a document sent to a prospective customer to secure business, sell products or get buy-in for an idea. A sales proposal follows a similar structure to a formal report but will be a more persuasive document.

There are several ingredients that help to create a persuasive proposal: it must back up any suggestions with arguments or fact; it must be creative, offering new ideas, rather than telling people what they already know; it must show an emotional commitment to the proposal; and it should demonstrate empathy, showing that you are aware of your readers' position and understand their problems, their markets and their business.

A sales proposal should follow a logical progression which captures the readers' attention right at the beginning, draws them in, poses the problem and then persuades them with a solution. It should follow this pattern:

- Establish common ground. Start off by showing you understand your readers. Put in some context: details of their business or the market in which they operate. This will make them feel comfortable and confident with you.

- Lay out the objectives: outline the reason you've been asked to put in this proposal, being aware all the time of your readers' perspective.

- Present the evidence: show them how you would achieve their goals.

- Deal with any likely resistance: it may be costs; it may be time taken; it may be what they can expect to achieve or receive. State everything now: it avoids awkward questions later.

- Underpin it with your strengths: why you are the best placed to do this, or why your product is the best for the job.

Structure of a sales proposal

Here is a typical structure for a sales proposal from a consultancy or agency; this structure can be adapted for different purposes and different business sectors:

- **Introduction**: Why are you writing this? What is the context? What can your reader expect?
- **Background**: Demonstrate your understanding of the reader: who they are, what they do, some facts about the market in which they operate, their competitors, and projects carried out in the past which are similar to this project.
- **Aims**: State what they are trying to achieve and why.
- **Strategy**: Give an overview of what you are proposing to do to achieve these aims.
- **Tactics**: Go into the details of how you will achieve them.
- **Deliverables and costs**: Explain precisely what they will receive and how much it will cost.
- **Evaluation**: Show how the programme will be measured.
- **About us**: Say who you are, who is in the team, your experience, and why they should use you.
- **Appendices**: Add any necessary background information needed to support points you have made.

Depending on the length of the proposal, you may also include a contents page and a summary (following the same procedure as you would for a standard report).

A sales proposal will use a numbering system in the same way as a report.

SALES PROPOSALS

Tone and language

Proposals should use the same tone and language as reports. They may also use graphics and diagrams to emphasize points more clearly than would be possible through words alone.

Checklist

- A sales proposal should be similar to a report in structure, style and tone.
- It differs from a report in that it is more persuasive, posing a problem and presenting the solution.

Business plans and programmes

What is a business plan?

A business plan is a document putting forward something new for internal or external use. It may cover several areas:

- an outline of a new business idea
- a strategy for growth
- a programme for a period of activities
- a rationale for change

In essence, a business plan is written in the same style as a report or proposal. It should be structured in logical, numbered sections; it should be written in an impersonal style; and it should use clear and concise language.

There are some key questions to ask before writing a business plan:

- Why am I writing this? What do I want to achieve as a result of this?
- Who will be reading this? What is their level of knowledge? How much do they need to know?
- What do I need to include: what facts are needed, and in how much detail should they be explained?
- What are the main points? Are there subsidiary areas which should be covered to support the main body of the plan?
- What supporting information is needed to back up the plan?

Structure of a business plan

A typical structure for a new business plan would be as follows:

- title page

BUSINESS PLANS AND PROGRAMMES

- contents page
- summary
- introduction: the new business idea in a nutshell
- rationale: the opportunity; the context; the current market
- the plan in detail: what the business would comprise; product or service details; staffing required; premises; marketing; etc
- finances: overview of pricing and likely profitability; costs; investment needed
- personnel: who is involved; their background and experience
- risks and threats
- next steps
- appendices: time plan; financial forecasts; company structure; etc

Checklist

- A business plan should be similar to a report in structure, style and tone.
- Keep in mind what it is you are trying to achieve and what your reader needs to know.

Electronic presentations

Supporting material

Electronic presentations are used to support speeches and spoken presentations. The key word here is *support*: all too often e-presentations are far too complex and the visuals simply replicate the spoken presentation. It is good practice to keep them as short as possible and use them simply to illustrate the key points of the spoken presentation. And remember: they are for the audience's benefit, not the presenter's.

An electronic presentation is in effect a summary of what you are saying. It will contain the key points, in the right order. It acts as a focal point for the audience, maintains their attention, and gives them reassurance that they are following what you are saying.

There is nothing worse than presenting an audience with a highly complicated and long slide: they won't read it and they will probably start to think about something else. A short, simple slide will hold their attention and keep them focused.

It is a good idea to take a two-stage approach to your preparation:

* First, put the slides together as notes for your presentation, and use that as the basis for deciding what you are going to say.
* Second, go back to your slides and shorten them, so that they really do just summarize your spoken presentation and keep the audience's attention.

Preparing an electronic presentation

This is not the place to go into great detail about the design of slides and the use of graphics, but here are some key points to bear in mind:

ELECTRONIC PRESENTATIONS

- Start with a title slide, showing the name of the presentation, the presenter and their organization.

- Have a summary slide at the beginning, outlining what you are going to say, and another one at the end, summarizing the main points.

- Use as few slides as possible. For a 30-minute presentation, the maximum should be ten and the goal should be six (a good rule of thumb is one slide every five minutes).

- Have only one topic on each slide.

- Use bullets for points rather than numbers, unless you are explaining a sequence.

- It's fine to use two columns of bulleted points but keep them really brief.

- Have a maximum of six or seven points with a maximum of seven words in each slide. If you are using a two-column format, the number of points can rise to twelve.

- Use upper-case for the first letter in each bulleted point, but otherwise avoid capitals except for abbreviations.

- Use simple, common typefaces.

- Avoid overuse of graphics: two per slide should be the maximum.

- Keep to a standard format for each slide: for example, have the company logo in the same place in each and use colour consistently.

- Suitable type-sizes are between 18 and 48 point. Try to use the same sizes for headings and body text throughout the presentation (for example, 36 point for headings and 22 point for body text).

- Don't overfill a slide: if it is bursting through the margins, either shorten it or split the information into two separate slides.

Examples

There are two examples of effective slides on page 127. The top slide is clear, concise and gives a brief summary of what you're talking about. The bottom slide shows a good way to end what seems like a pitch for business, with a suitably light-hearted ending.

Press Relations

What does the press want?

⌘ timely access to interesting, articulate experts and stories

⌘ newsworthy and usable releases

⌘ unbiased, well-written articles

Next steps

⌘ Agree terms

⌘ Meet February 5th

⌘ Put plan together

⌘ Get cracking!

Practice exercise

1 The top slide on page 128 contains far too much information. It contains almost the entire content of what is going to be given orally and needs to be cut back. Make it shorter and lay it out more clearly.

2 The bottom slide has some interesting things to say, but it is far

too complex. Rework it to make it clearer. Compare your versions of both slides with the ones on page 194.

How to proceed – one view

Top 10 Tips

- ⌘ Get both senior buy-in and grass roots support – early
- ⌘ Go global if you can – otherwise you'll end up with multiple communities, policies and branding
- ⌘ Map the benefits against your brand values and make sure there's a fit
- ⌘ Set clear objectives – work out what you want to achieve and plan accordingly
- ⌘ Make the business decisions first – the technology should follow
- ⌘ Being the first in your sector can give you unexpected PR and business advantage
- ⌘ Don't wait for everything to be perfect before you launch – chances are it never will be, and you'll miss your window of opportunity
- ⌘ Don't underestimate the time required after launch to nurture and prune
- ⌘ Put guidelines and a code of practice in place – and make them visible to visitors
- ⌘ Don't be afraid to experiment – on a small scale

Managing complex change

	+ skills	+ incentive	+ resources	+ action plan	= confusion
vision		+ incentive	+ resources	+ action plan	= anxiety
vision	+ skills	+ incentive	+ resources		
vision	+ skills	+ incentive		+ action plan	= false starts
vision	+ skills		+ resources	+ action plan	= gradual change
vision	+ skills	+ incentive	+ resources	+ action plan	= change

Checklist

- Keep presentation slides short and simple.
- Slides should summarize the key points.
- Aim to use one slide for every five minutes of a presentation.
- Have one topic per slide.
- Aim for a maximum of six or seven points on each slide.

Part Three
Marketing and Corporate Communications

MARKETING AND CORPORATE COMMUNICATIONS

There are some written business communications which are usually the responsibility of specialists: either specialists within your organization, or external bodies such as PR consultancies or marketing agencies. This section is aimed at giving you an overview of how these more sophisticated communications should be written. It will equip you to comment on their content and composition in a practical and informed way.

Press releases

What is a press release?

A press release is a news story issued by an organization announcing something it would like to be covered by the media. The key word here is *news*: press releases should only be issued if they contain information on something new. This may be a new product, service or customer; it may also be new information such as the results of a survey, the receiving of an award, an achievement by an employee, or the effects of a new product or service on a customer.

It is important to take an objective view. The story must be of interest to its targets and not just to the organization issuing it. The key is to subject it to the 'So what?' test. Is it really of interest to anyone outside your organization? How will a journalist react to it? And remember: press releases should only be sent to media whose *audience* – the people who read, watch or listen to it – is interested in your story.

The aim of a press release is to achieve coverage. A press release is a communication between an organization and its specific target audience (prospects, customers, investors, etc) which uses the media as the vehicle to carry that communication. A press release is not aimed at communicating *with* the press; it is aimed at communicating *via* the press.

A good press release should have these qualities:

- It should be usable by the media in its entirety and exactly as it is written: it should therefore be written in a style that would be found in a newspaper or magazine.
- It must be issued at the right time: when the news is at its strongest and most relevant. Speed is of the essence: if you have

something new and exciting to say, then make sure you release it as soon as you can.

- The news must be clear: make sure you are telling only *one* news story at a time and that the recipient can understand exactly what that story is.

- It must gain the journalist's attention immediately: publications and other media outlets receive hundreds of press releases a week, by post, e-mail or fax. Yours will be just one of them. So you have to maximize its chance of being noticed and read. That's why it's vital to follow the accepted structure (which is set out below). Only then will it stand any chance of being noticed.

- It must be written in a suitable style and tone: a news release is written for use by journalists and therefore should be written in a journalistic style. This means no ridiculous claims (such as *the world's leading organization* or *the biggest and best product*). It has to be factual; any claims must be substantiated. Avoid hype, avoid adjectives, and avoid flowery, emotive language.

- Only include information you are happy to see published: all information should be verified and approved by anyone implicated.

Structure of a press release

A successful press release should follow an 'inverted triangle' format. The most important information goes first and information decreases in importance as the release continues. In fact, you should be able to cut the finished press release from the end upwards, paragraph by paragraph, and the remaining copy should still communicate the story you want to tell.

It is crucial to have a heading that grabs the attention. This is your only chance to hook the journalist. The heading should contain the core news in a short, succinct sentence so that the journalist reading it is encouraged to read on.

The paragraph that follows the heading must contain the bare facts of the story: if it doesn't, the journalist will simply move on to the next release in the in-box. Journalists are interested in the 'five Ws': *who* is releasing the story; *what* the story is about; *when* it happened; *where* it happened; and *why* this is different or important. The opening paragraph should be able to stand by itself without any supporting information.

The subsequent paragraphs should then develop the story, giving more information on the news, supporting the first paragraph and expanding on it.

Include one or two quotes in these paragraphs. A quote can contain opinion and comment that is more promotional than the rest of the press release. The quotes should be from relevant people, such as a representative of someone featured in the release (perhaps the customer, the central figure in the news) and/or the managing director of the organization issuing the release. The quotes should illuminate the story and add a bit of colour.

The press release should finish with background information about the organizations mentioned in it. This is commonly known as the 'boilerplate' and is usually a standard paragraph that will not change from one press release to another.

Finally, include relevant details needed by the press: these should include the date of issue, the name and contact details of the person available to give more information, and other useful facts such as whether there are photos available.

Within this structure, the following guidelines apply:
- Each paragraph should contain no more than four sentences.
- Sentences should be short and concise, with one idea per sentence. If a sentence is too long, split it up into two shorter sentences.
- The release as a whole should be short – never more than two pages.

PRESS RELEASES

Example

There is an example of a clear, concise and successful press release on page 137. Notice the following points:

* It clearly states the subject in the heading.
* The first paragraph communicates the five Ws and could stand alone to give the gist of the story.
* The subsequent paragraphs support the first paragraph and build the story.
* There is an interesting and relevant quote which illuminates the story.
* There is a suitable boilerplate plus useful details.
* It is written in an objective way, with no superlatives or unsubstantiated claims.

Reviewing press releases

If you are asked to review a press release, ask yourself the following questions:

* Does the heading grab your attention and tell you what the story is about?
* Does the first paragraph contain the five Ws: *who*, *what*, *when*, *where* and *why*?
* Does the press release have a single message and present this in a clear and coherent way?
* Does it use suitable language so that it could be reproduced in a newspaper or magazine?
* Does it contain any unsubstantiated or biased claims that need to be removed?
* Does it contain any statements that give a negative impression of the organization?

INSTANTCASH ATMs INCREASE
FOOTFALL AND SALES AT CENTRE NEWS

Increased footfall and customer spend are being experienced by Centre News as a result of installing cash machines in its convenience stores. The organization is now rolling out ATMs from independent deployer InstantCash across its network of community stores.

Centre News has almost 200 outlets, predominantly in the Midlands. The majority are newsagents but these are gradually being upgraded to convenience stores. The first InstantCash ATMs were installed in late 2006 and there is already a noticeable increase in footfall and sales.

ATMs are also providing Centre News with an extra revenue stream through a share of the convenience fee. Customers are charged £1.50 per withdrawal and Centre has experienced a positive reaction to this: customers recognize it as another convenient service for which they are willing to pay.

Centre News believes ATMs add value to the customers' shopping experience and are particularly convenient in its community sites. These tend to be on housing estates, away from high-street banks. In addition, they offer enhanced security when withdrawing cash, particularly for women.

Peter Ridge, Head of Retail Services for Centre News, is delighted with the results of installing ATMs from InstantCash: 'It's obvious in many stores that more people are coming in because of the cash machine. And every time we've put an ATM into a store, sales have increased. This, coupled with the convenience fee, is contributing to our profitability. We've been very impressed with the service offered by InstantCash and believe it offers the perfect package for a multi-site operator.'

(ends)

InstantCash is an independent ATM deployer and member of the LINK interchange network. Based in Bristol, its customers include Dry Leisure, Moon TV, Smith & Son and the FS Group. For more information, visit www.instantcash.net

For more press information, contact:
Sally Poole, 01211 522222, pr@prcom
26 April 2007

PRESS RELEASES

- Press releases should contain information about something new.
- They should follow an inverted triangle format, with the key information in the first paragraph.
- They should be suitably journalistic in tone.
- Quotes can be used to add colour and personal comment.

Leaflets and brochures

What is it for?

A leaflet or brochure is usually used to communicate an organization's sales messages. The written element of such a document is only one aspect of it: equally important are the design and the material on which it is printed.

A leaflet or brochure is a stand-alone piece of marketing material and should be complete and aimed at achieving a single purpose. Its aim is to inform, educate and persuade, and ultimately encourage an action: usually a purchase or a further enquiry.

As a starting point, the key messages which are being communicated need to be agreed, and these should then permeate the brochure copy. They are likely to focus on the unique selling points (USPs) of the products or services – what makes them different from others on the market. A USP may be quality, price, availability, longevity or depth of range available, or a combination of these points.

Who is it for?

As ever, the most important person to keep in mind is the recipient. So always ask yourself:

- What do they want to know?
- How much information do they already have?
- How much needs to be explained?
- How many different types of people will read the brochure and how can it meet their different needs?
- How detailed or technical does it need to be?

LEAFLETS AND BROCHURES

Planning a brochure

The best way to start planning brochure content is to produce an outline of the different sections. This will not only help to gather thoughts and facts but will also feed into the layout and help decide how long it should be.

The following outline might be suitable for a brochure advertising a range of products for the business market:

* title, subheading, slogan or company strapline
* overview of subject matter: summary of the range and its benefits to the user
* product range in detail
* products in action: some case studies
* support services available
* company background and history
* profiles of sales staff
* contact details

A leaflet for a hotel might require a different outline:

* hotel name and strapline
* general description of hotel including key facilities and location
* accommodation
* restaurant
* leisure facilities
* management team
* nearby attractions
* prices
* contact details and map

Producing this sort of simple outline focuses thoughts on what needs to be included and how long the brochure should be. It can also be used as the basis for a provisional design. The content can now be built up around these different headings.

Style and tone

Here are some guidelines on what makes good copy for a brochure:

- Brochures should be easy to read and broken down into manageable sections. Use plenty of headings, subheadings and bulleted points to take the reader logically through the text.

- Only include what is absolutely necessary: the shorter the brochure, the easier it is to communicate its messages. Ask yourself: 'Is this really needed? Will the brochure suffer if we take it out?'

- Don't overwhelm the reader with words. A short and simple brochure will be easy to read. Use images instead of words wherever possible.

- Remember that you are trying to persuade someone to do something as a result of reading the brochure. So make the text lively and interesting. Use descriptive adjectives and adverbs.

You can see these principles in action in this example:

> *Since its foundation in 1988, Intersafe has spearheaded network and information security. It is now Europe's leading security systems integrator, the trusted security partner for over 50 per cent of the FTSE 100, and employs some of the most skilled engineers in the industry.*

Notice the use of powerful words such as *spearheaded*. Unlike press releases, brochures can use persuasive words such as *leading*, *trusted* and *most skilled*.

This next example also shows descriptive language can make good promotional copy:

> *The Cranford Park Hotel stands in exquisite grounds laid out in the 18th century by famed garden designer*

LEAFLETS AND BROCHURES

> *Capability Brown. With colourful flower beds and magnificent tree-lined paths, it offers an oasis of calm and a magical experience for visitors and guests.*

This really paints a picture and draws the reader in. Note how the use of adjectives such as *exquisite*, *colourful*, *magnificent* and *magical* bring it to life.

Reviewing brochure copy

If you are asked to review brochure copy, ask yourself the following questions:

* If I were the intended recipient, what picture would the copy paint for me?
* Does it tell me everything I need to know in order to make the required decision?
* Does it make me more likely to make that decision than if I hadn't read it?
* Does it take me through the content logically or do I have to keep jumping around?
* Is the copy interesting and persuasive?
* Is it just too long? Does it get boring? Do I really need to read all this?
* Do the sales messages come through clearly? Does it really communicate what our organization is trying to say?

Checklist

* Leaflets and brochures should communicate an organization's key messages.
* Keep in mind the requirements of the recipients.
* Use plenty of headings, subheadings and bulleted points to take the reader logically through the text.
* Use descriptive words to make the text lively and interesting.

Direct mail

Direct mail letters are written to inform and persuade, and the intention is usually to prompt action. They are often sent unsolicited and are therefore often received with suspicion or hostility, so they need to be compellingly written to have any impact and to succeed in their objective.

The hostility with which it is likely to be greeted makes it all the more vital that a direct mail letter has an instant impact: if not it will simply go in the bin. So a direct mail letter must *immediately* draw its readers in and make them want to read on.

All the same rules apply to direct mail letters as they do to standard business letters (see pages 81–7). But there is a useful and now widely accepted formula for structuring direct mail letters which helps to make them more powerful and persuasive. This entails planning them in four sections which follow the acronym AIDA (Attention, Interest, Desire, Action).

A – Attention
The first task is to grab the attention of the readers, to hook them in and ensure they read on. This may take the form of a powerful heading; it may be a strongly worded and compelling first paragraph; or it may be a combination of these. This can be achieved by:

* asking a question to which the reader's most likely answer is *yes*
* stating a fact which they will find extraordinary
* referring to something which is particularly relevant to them

I – Interest
The next section needs to confirm this interest, by capitalizing on and expanding whatever had initially captured their attention. This may be achieved by:

- expanding on the first point and giving more information
- introducing something new which will make them even more interested
- saying something that makes them think, 'This sounds fantastic!'
- saying something that makes them think, 'This has really highlighted a problem I face'

D – Desire

Having captured their attention and made them interested, you now need to deliver the killer punch by presenting something which they really want to have or to know. This may be:

- a new or relevant product or service
- a special offer which makes something even more interesting or relevant than normal
- an opportunity which they just cannot refuse
- a solution to a problem

A – Action

By persuading them that they really want whatever is on offer, you now need to make it easy for them to act on this desire and obtain it. So tell them how to proceed by stating:

- whom they need to contact
- how they need to make that contact
- the deadline, if appropriate
- what they should expect in return

PS

And finally, try to use a PS. This gives you the opportunity to put something which grabs their attention at the foot of the letter. The reader's eye is naturally drawn to a PS, so exploit it: put in a special offer, or extra information which makes the letter even more compelling.

Personalization

The very best direct mail letter sounds as if it is a one-off: a letter written by a real person to one recipient alone. If possible, a direct mail letter should be personalized: this means it should be sent to a named individual and have some form of personal reference within the body of the letter itself. This makes it more compelling and more likely to achieve success.

In many instances, of course, this degree of personalization is just not practical. However, another good way of personalizing a direct mail letter is to have a real signature at the end. If this is practical, it can make all the difference between success and oblivion.

Length and tone

Try to keep a direct mail letter on one page. Keep paragraphs short, and sentences sharp and concise, using clear but compelling language. Most of all, make it personal: write it as you would a personal letter to someone.

E-broadcasts

An e-broadcast is a direct mail letter sent by e-mail. There are strict rules over the legality of e-mail marketing, within the Privacy and Electronic Communications (EC Directive) Regulations 2003, which lay down who can and cannot be e-mailed without their consent. This is vital information for any direct marketer.

If it is to be carried out (legally), then the guidelines for successful e-broadcasts are exactly the same as for paper-based direct mail, but applied to an e-mail format:

* If you have someone in the organization who is known to the recipients, then use them as the sender. If not, send it from the company.

* Have a compelling subject line: something that is relevant and interesting.

* If possible, personalize it. It is amazing how much more attention people pay to an e-mail if it is addressed personally to them: it

makes it seem like a one-off.

* If possible, put something personal in the text: this could be the name of their organization, an event they have attended, or something they have bought in the past.

* Follow the AIDA format: this will hook them in, keep them interested and prompt them to action.

* Keep it short: keep paragraphs short; keep sentences short; keep language sharp and concise.

Example
On page 147 there is a good example of a direct-mail letter designed to be used as an e-broadcast which follows the AIDA format.

Reviewing direct mail
When reviewing a piece of direct mail – either paper-based or electronic – ask yourself these questions:

* Do I feel it is addressed to me personally?

* Does it capture my attention in a compelling way immediately?

* Does it then make me want to find out more and therefore read on?

* Does it offer me something that will satisfy this interest?

* Does it clearly explain what I need to do next?

Checklist

* It is essential to capture the reader's attention immediately.
* Use the AIDA format: Attention, Interest, Desire, Action.
* Add a personal detail if you can.

Dear Mr Khan

Do you face demands from staff, suppliers or customers for web access to critical information?

Is the value of your legacy systems maximized within a modern IT infrastructure?

Are your disparate applications really communicating across the entire business?

And do you have the resources to cope with these challenges? That's where Zenith can offer support.

From time to time, your in-house IT skills may not be sufficient. You may come up against a complex technical problem; you may need extra resources; or you could simply benefit from outside advice and a different perspective.

My company, Zenith, offers a rare combination: a systems integration consultancy which solves your technology challenges based on a clear business understanding. Our highly experienced team will ensure your IT infrastructure genuinely fits around your business – and not the other way around.

We can step in when you need us: to complement your own team or work independently, to address resourcing issues or to brainstorm a specific IT concern.

We would like to explain further the advantages of working with Zenith. Click here to find out more about our services and our past successes, how we could work together, or to ask for one of our team to contact you.

Yours sincerely

Peter Cain

Newsletters can be a great way to communicate with a target audience on a regular basis in a slightly informal way. The key to their success is to make sure they are of interest to their targets and contain compelling and useful snippets of information.

As the name implies, a newsletter is a combination of a *news* story and a *letter*: it should contain news but also feel personal. It should be written in a journalistic style and contain information of current interest, but at the same time feel as if it is addressed to the readers themselves. This may even take the form of starting with *Dear Customer* or a similar form of address.

Newsletters can be used for a variety of purposes, for example to communicate with employees, members, special interest groups, prospects, customers and stakeholders. The readership will dictate the content: this should always focus on issues which are of interest to them.

Styles can vary slightly according to the audience, but fundamentally newsletters should be:

- **Personal**: There should be a personal tone to them, which draws the reader in. Newsletters are a great way of humanizing an organization and giving it a face. It's perfectly acceptable to talk in terms of 'we' and 'you'.
- **Human**: Humour and human-interest stories will add life and colour.
- **Regular**: Newsletters are never one-off – they are part of a continuing series. So establish a style to create familiarity and make readers feel part of it. Once a style is created and it has gained reader approval, stick with it.
- **Sustainable**: It may be easy enough to find material for the first

or second edition, but can this be sustained? Is there enough information to warrant a regular newsletter on a long-term basis?

- **Written in a journalistic style**: Articles should be short, so readers can 'dip in' without too many demands on their time and attention. In addition, articles should follow the inverted triangle style used for press releases: the first paragraph should contain the key facts (the five Ws) and you should be able to cut from the end of the article upwards.

- **Balanced between marketing and journalism**: On the one hand, newsletters should convey corporate marketing or sales messages; on the other hand, they should appear independent and useful. Judging this balance is best left to specialists but beware losing focus by moving too far in either direction.

Good content for newsletters might include:

- an editorial or comment from a senior person: written in the first person and giving personal opinion
- news stories on staff, customers, associates, events and awards
- external, background news stories which are relevant to the readership
- progress on previous stories: updates on what's happened since the last newsletter
- in-depth profiles, such as a customer case-study or an article about a particular member of staff
- calendars of events
- competitions
- quizzes

Examples

There are some good examples of newsletter content on page 150:

NEWSLETTERS

London Marathon time is approaching, and the Timecom team is pounding the countryside around Beaconsfield en masse to avoid the loneliness of the long-distance runner. We're well on target to raise £100,000 for local charities through a series of events and sponsorship: there's one in particular which readers might like to take part in (see page 11). We'll report on how much we raise – and our blistered feet – in the next issue of Time IT.

Woks were sizzling and knives gleaming in the lightbulbs as celebrity chef Jim Thompson opened C&R's new in-house eating experience, The Food Stop. In true TV chef style, Jim prepared food for the assembled multitude, entertaining the crowds as he chopped and fried. The Food Stop promises to be a unique and innovative food experience and we look forward to welcoming you there in the near future.

Reviewing newsletters

When reviewing newsletter copy, ask yourself the following questions:

- Is it likely to appeal to its intended readership or is it too focused on items which are only of interest to the writer?
- Is there sufficient variety to offer something of interest to everyone?
- Is it easy to dip in and read individual items?
- Would I learn anything about the issuing organization as a result of reading this?
- Would I look forward to receiving the next issue?

Checklist

- Write in a journalistic style.
- Focus on issues which are of interest to the target readers.
- Establish a particular style and stick to it.

Websites

Every organization is now likely to have a website. It is the window through which it is viewed by the world – literally. So it's all the more important that it communicates effectively.

To create the very best website – and to ensure the copy within it is right – you should start by thinking how visitors will use the site and what they're looking for. And the key to this is to remember one thing above all others: people do not like reading on the Web. It's not the most conducive way of reading: it tires the eyes.

Instead, they scan the page and pick out the important points. If they want to read something substantive, they will go elsewhere. So what's important is that you make it easy for them to scan.

Making a good, quick impact is vital. Whether they are just surfing or have specifically looked for your site, visitors will want to know immediately what the site is about, to help them make the decision to read on. Even then, they want to assimilate your messages quickly as they navigate their way through your site.

So the key to good copy for websites is a strong first impression coupled with brevity, so the reader can see immediately what the page is about and quickly get the gist of the content. Then, if they want, they can read the whole thing in more detail.

The first impression isn't just about the copy, of course. It's also about the design of the page, the layout of the copy, the ease of navigation and the technology you deploy. Some sites suffer from being too clever, with amazing animations and graphics which simply delay or distract – or perhaps don't even work at all. The best sites opt for a combination of simplicity and professionalism designed to help the visitor to read, understand and come back for more.

151

WEBSITES

Tone, structure and length

The language used on websites should be clear and simple. Follow the usual basic rules, but keep in mind the special requirements of the Web:

- Pay special attention to keeping sentences and paragraphs short.
- There should be plenty of headings, subheadings and bullet points. These make it easy for readers: they can see at a glance what the page is about, what the main points are and which sections they really want to read.
- Don't use numbered bullets unless the information is in order of importance.
- Pages should be short: try to avoid having so much copy that it disappears off the bottom of the screen. Visitors should be able to see everything in the one window. If the page is too long, think about cutting it back and putting the extra copy on a lower-ranked, linked page.
- Highlight key information – single words or short phrases – to make them stand out when the reader scans. One highlighted phrase in each paragraph works well.
- Be objective: write for the reader, not for the organization. Avoid superlatives and overstated claims.

The home page

The home page has to be treated differently from the rest of the site. This is your 'front door': and it should be welcoming and enticing. While still following the same style as the rest of the site, it will be very different in content and layout. It should give a very brief indication of what the site is all about – two paragraphs at most. It should not have long sections of copy telling you everything on the site. It's more like a combination of a lively title and contents page, with easy links to the rest of the site. Brevity is key.

Some good examples of corporate home pages can be found at these Web addresses:

http://www.blackandwhitecommunications.com
http://www.iwebsharedealing.co.uk
http://www.chewtonglen.co.uk

Reviewing web copy

When reviewing web copy, ask yourself the following questions:

- Does the home page draw me in? Does it make me want to explore further into the site?

- Does the home page give me a good idea of what this site is about?

- Are the pages easy to read? Can I scan them to get a good idea of the main points?

- Do I believe what it's saying?

- Does it convey the right messages about our organization? What would I feel about this organization if I visited this site?

Checklist

- Your website should create a strong first impression on visitors.

- Make it easy for readers to see at a glance what each page is about.

- Pay special attention to keeping sentences and paragraphs short.

Financial communications

This is a realm that really *must* be left to professionals. Financial communications demand a combination of accounting skills and writing skills, tempered by strict regulations laid down by organizations such as the Financial Services Authority. Recent high-profile court cases have highlighted the folly of making statements about financial performance which might mislead the market. Whether done unintentionally or deliberately, the penalties for misleading statements can be very harsh.

If you work for a publicly quoted company, any public communications can have an effect on the share price. Therefore every written communication should theoretically be checked by an expert who understands what can and cannot be stated in public. This may not happen in practice, and this poses a considerable risk.

The answer is to leave it to the experts: your financial PR and investor relations advisers.

Part Four

Perfecting Your Work

PERFECTING YOUR WORK

There are three distinct aspects to creating a piece of writing. Firstly, you need to plan it: research it, gather your thoughts and then decide how the piece will be structured. Secondly, you need to write it: go through a first draft and then rework it or shorten it until it meets the brief. And thirdly, you need to make sure it has no mistakes and is a consistent piece of writing. This section will take you through those three steps.

Planning and drafting

When you are writing an extended piece of work – for example a lengthy report, a presentation or a proposal – it needs to have a clear and coherent structure, which means it needs to be well thought out from the start. By the time you have thought about your objectives and completed any research, you should have a clear idea of what you are setting out to do. You now need to draw up a plan of how to do it.

Your plan needs to have a clear structure, allowing you to introduce information and ideas in a logical order. There are many possible approaches. However, most plans should start with three clearly identifiable parts:

* an **introduction**, in which you state what you are intending to do and why you are doing it
* a **main body** containing information, arguments and evidence
* a **conclusion**, in which you summarize what you have previously said, and state clearly any conclusions or recommendations

Converting research notes into a plan

Within this general structure, you need to arrange the particular things you want to say in your document. This can be done in a few easy stages:

* Write down all of the arguments or points that you have assembled during the course of your research. At this stage, all you need is a brief note of each point.
* Try to collect these arguments into groups under a series of general headings.
* Now try to fit the general headings together into the most logical order. If there are arguments for and against something, group all of the arguments for it together, then group all of the arguments

against it together. Do not bounce backwards and forwards between the two.

- Make sure the order you have come up with fulfils your original goals. If there are any obvious gaps in the order, you may need to go back and do more research to fill these in.

It is a good idea to start with a simple outline and move on to something more complex, fleshing out the bones only once you have built the skeleton. Do not be afraid to cross things out and move them around as you develop your plan – that is what this stage of the process is all about.

Lateral thinking

If you find it difficult to organize your thoughts, put aside the approach mentioned above, and see instead whether any more lateral ways of organizing your material emerge from the material itself. Here are a few techniques you might try:

- Write a key word or underlying idea in the middle of a large sheet of paper, then write related words and ideas all over the sheet, drawing lines from the centre to related items, as well as between related items, to form a web or network of connected ideas. This might lead to something like this:

France	Services
Popularity	Hotels
Differences from UK	Vineyards
What's on offer	Markets
	Sites

French route planning service

UK travellers	Stories
Types	Families
Times	Couples
Needs	Singles

- Write single words or ideas on index cards and lay them out on the floor, arranging related items into groups or piles.

- Use question words such as *who*, *why*, *where*, *when* and *how* to generate possible ideas for approaches to the topic. Imagine the questions your readers would ask you if they had the opportunity to speak to you in person.

Once you have decided what the key ideas or points are, assess their relative importance, and decide in what order you want to deal with them. There may be several different ways of arranging your material. What is important is that your plan covers all of the material and that it provides a clear structure for what you have to say.

Your final plan may look something like this:

Introduction: The idea of a route planning service

Main body

1. What is it about France?
   a) Popularity
   b) Challenges for travellers
2. UK travellers
   a) Who are they?
   b) When do they go?
   c) What do they need?
3. Route planning services
   a) Roads
   b) Vineyards, markets and sites
4. Experiences
   a) Families
   b) Couples
   c) Singles

Conclusion: what we've learnt and where we go from here.

PLANNING AND DRAFTING

Having established a basic plan, you may wish to expand this into a more detailed plan, or you may wish to move on immediately to your first draft of the document.

Traditionally, at this early stage writers used pen and paper to create a plan, adding notes and crossing things out as they went. However, word processors now make it easy to put down a mass of ideas, and then reorder them by dragging blocks of text around the screen to build up a structure. Whichever method you are using, do not be afraid to change your mind – it is better to make alterations to your plan early rather than at a later stage when things are more settled and difficult to change.

Drafting – getting started

Once you have come up with a plan that meets your aims for your document, you are ready to start writing. You are now confronted with one of the most off-putting sights for a writer: a blank sheet of paper, or an empty computer screen. It is a good idea to get over this stage as quickly as possible, so make a start without assuming that the first thing you write will necessarily still be there in your final version. The important thing is to get started – it is far easier to make changes once you have something to work with, rather than wasting time staring anxiously at an empty screen and wondering what to do. In short, just do it!

Drafting – filling out the plan

Once you start to write, you should find that the preparation work you have done pays off, and the writing begins to flow more easily.

Keep in mind the following points as you write:

- Follow the plan you have drawn up. It would be a shame to waste all the work that went into producing it, and the plan will help you to organize your ideas.

- Do not think you have to complete a paragraph before moving on. If you get stuck, go on to the next one and come back later. You will then be able to look at it with fresh eyes and perhaps see what needs to be changed. If you are really stuck, delete the whole paragraph and start again.

- It is likely that new ideas and insights will occur to you as you write. If new ideas present themselves, do not be afraid to 'go with the flow' and change what you are doing to take account of them – provided that they can be accommodated within your plan.

- Try to deal proportionately with the various different points and arguments. Don't spend a long period on a single point and then skirt around other points that are more important.

- Think about the people who will be reading the document and try to make life easy for them. If people are going to use the document to retrieve information, think about making it easy to scan by using headings, lists and tables. If people are going to read it as a continuous piece, make sure that it is divided up into manageable paragraphs and that there is a coherent and logical structure.

- If you make a statement or express an opinion, back this up with evidence in the form of facts and figures or quotations. However, use facts and figures selectively and appropriately. Don't overwhelm your readers with them.

Checklist

- Plan the structure before you start to write any complex piece of writing.

- Once you have a plan, go ahead and start writing – don't worry about whether what you write will be good enough for your final version.

- Follow the plan you have drawn up.

Revising and reworking

General revising

Once you have finished a single complete version of your document, you have the opportunity to change and improve it. It is usually more helpful to produce something that is complete but imperfect and then revise that, rather than wasting time trying to produce something that is perfect first time.

Check that all the points in your plan have been covered in a logical order, and that everything you have included is in fact necessary to your argument.

Check also that you have dealt with each issue clearly, and that you move smoothly from one point to the next. If you have not done this, add extra material to explain, introduce or summarize where necessary, as this will make your work more polished.

Once you are satisfied with the overall structure and content, you can concentrate on getting the introduction and the conclusion right. You may find that what you originally said in your introduction is no longer valid because you have made changes during the writing process. Now is the time to get it right.

Checking the details

If you are happy that your document is well-organized and coherent as a whole, you can turn your attention to the details: check the seven Cs, making sure your writing is:

- **Correct**: There should be no errors in facts, spelling, grammar or punctuation.
- **Consistent**: Things should be expressed in the same way each time you refer to them, and you should follow the same style and

the same layout throughout.

- **Clear**: The language should be easy to read, the information be easy to understand, and text be attractively laid out, with plenty of space and enough headings to help your readers – but not so many that they interrupt the flow of the document.
- **Complete**: All of the relevant material should be included, including explanations of unfamiliar terms and abbreviations, any background information, and acknowledgement of your sources.
- **Concise**: The information should be presented in the simplest and most direct way possible.
- **Courteous**: The tone should be polite, and there should be no words which will offend or alienate.
- **Careful**: Nothing should be capable of misconstruction, nothing should be overstated, and everything should be justified.

Shortening

Sometimes you have to work to a specified word-count, or you have to shorten your previous work for another use.

The first thing to look for are unnecessary words. Delete any words that could be omitted without changing the meaning of the sentence:

    ✗ *The subject of writing skills in business is something of a challenge.*

    ✔ *Writing skills in business is a challenge.*

It may also be that you can combine phrases or replace longer phrases with a single word:

    ✗ *Often the practical aspect is considered the crucial element.*

    ✔ *Often the practical aspect is crucial.*

Besides cutting out unnecessary words, you might also try turning passive sentences around by changing the subject and making them active:

> ✗ *The sector also has a well-established set of professional awards, where individual campaigns are praised and applauded for their originality.*

> ✔ *Professional awards praise individual campaigns for their originality.*

Finally, be objective and remove phrases which may add colour but are not vital to the overall sense:

> ✗ *This is not an exhaustive study of the subject: there are many other examples we could have included.*

> ✔ *This is not an exhaustive study of the subject.*

Summarizing

Summarizing is a different process to shortening: a summary needs to convey the vital points of the document in as succinct a format as possible. Summaries are particularly important in long documents such as reports, proposals or plans, where you want to give the reader an opportunity to understand the entire document in as short a time as possible.

Here are the steps to take to achieve successful summaries:

* Before you start, make sure you are really familiar with the entire document. Read it through several times.
* Think of it from the point of view of the reader: what are the main points that you would want them to take from the document?
* Make notes of these main points.
* There may be sentences within the body of the document which would work well in the summary: if so, cut and paste into the summary, and then shorten if necessary using the techniques described above.
* Don't simply string together summaries of each paragraph: consider whole sections and summarize those.
* Once you have written the summary, reread your notes on the main points and check that they are all covered.

- Read the summary and judge whether it stands alone as a self-contained piece of writing. Make sure you are not making any presumptions on knowledge or that any statements you make only work if you have read the full document.

Practice exercise

Look at the report on pages 117–18. Write a summary of it in no more than 75 words. Compare your version with the one on page 195.

Checklist

- It is easier to produce something that is imperfect and then revise that, rather than trying to produce something that is perfect first time.

- Make sure your writing follows the seven Cs: correct, consistent, clear, complete, concise, courteous and careful.

- You may be able to shorten a document that is too long by removing unnecessary words and by rewriting sentences.

- Summarizing is not the same as shortening: a summary should include all the key points of a document.

Proofreading

How to proofread

There's no point in producing great written work if it is riddled with spelling and typing mistakes. This section will look at the steps you can take to review your work and make sure it is correct and consistent.

Proofreading is a vital part of the writing process. It should take place at the very end of the process: after any editing, which may allow errors to creep in again; and immediately before you send or present the written communication.

Here are some guidelines for successful proofreading:

* If you are proofreading your own work, don't do it immediately after you've written it. Take a break from it before you start to proofread. It is difficult to have an independent perspective on something that is so familiar to you. So put it aside, do something else, and then start the proofreading process later.

* Find a quiet place to proofread, away from distractions. This is a task that needs your full concentration.

* If the document you are working on is long, then proofread in short, concentrated sessions and take frequent breaks (but remember to mark where you have paused in the text).

* Make sure you are well acquainted with your house style, if you have one.

* Use the medium which works best for you: if you prefer reading on paper, then print the document out; if you are happy with reading on screen, then work on a computer.

* It can help to change the look of the document: for example, if you are working in Microsoft Word, change from normal view to reading or print layout when you start proofreading.

- As you read the text, 'hear' it inside your head (or even read it out aloud): this can really help with comprehension.

- Never, ever rely on spellcheckers: these will indicate words which are wrongly spelt but will not tell you if they are in the wrong context.

- Likewise, do not rely on grammar checkers: these can be quite flaky.

- Proofread slowly and look for one error at a time.

- Take the text one sentence at a time. Read a sentence once for sense and then reread it for errors. Sometimes, when reading a document for sense, the brain believes it has read something which is correct when in fact it is an error.

- When searching for errors, it can sometimes even help to read a document backwards: this ensures you are only focusing on errors and not on the sense.

- Know your weaknesses: if there are certain errors which you tend to miss, then pay particular attention to these.

House style

Proofreading should pay attention to house style – a set of rules for ensuring consistency in the use of English throughout an organization. Having a consistent style conveys a professional image to clients, but it is important that it is adopted in *every* communication, from the most informal e-mail to the most crucial report or client proposal. If you use it constantly, it should become second nature and you will start to apply it automatically.

A style guide should answer the following points:

- Which spelling should be used when there is a choice of several acceptable spellings?
- Which words can be abbreviated, and in what form?
- Which words should be written with foreign accents?
- When are capital letters and italics to be used?
- What style should be used to show dates and numbers?

PROOFREADING

It may also cover areas such as:

* How should lists be set out?
* Should single or double inverted commas be used to indicate speech?
* How should foreign or technical words be written?

Some suggestions about suitable style can be found on pages 171–9. But if your organization has its own house style you must stick to that.

What to look for when proofreading

It is all very well to read a piece of writing looking for mistakes, but what exactly should you be watching out for? Here is a list of the sort of things that can go wrong in a piece of writing. In fact, we have covered many of these elsewhere in this book:

* using unnecessary or repetitive words (see pages 24–7)
* words being used in the wrong place (see pages 54–74)
* missing and incorrect punctuation (see pages 37–53)
* spelling errors: if in doubt, consult a dictionary
* inconsistencies, particularly in points governed by house style
* incorrect double letters in words such as *targetted*, *combatting*, *focussing*, *skillfull*
* missing words: it's easy for the eyes and brain to assume that a word is there when it's not, so read slowly and don't skim
* missing letters in words: it's easy for the eyes and brain to assume a word is correct, so read slowly and look at each word in isolation
* extra words, in particular short words such as *the*, *a* and *to*: these often creep into documents as a result of previous changes
* extra letters in words: particularly three letters being typed instead of a double letter
* incorrect facts: verify figures, percentages, the spelling of proper names, telephone numbers, etc

How to make corrections

Here are some guidelines for making simple text corrections:

* To delete material, cross it out with a single line and put *delete* or a delta sign (♪) in the margin.
* To restore material deleted in error, underscore it with a dotted line and write *stet* in the margin.
* Always put new material in the margin, not in the text itself.
* To add material, place a caret mark (⅃) in the appropriate place in the text and also in the margin next to the new text.
* If additional material will not fit in the margin, type it on an additional sheet and clearly reference it in the margin.
* To prevent confusion, do not use block capitals unless the text you are inserting is in capitals.
* Write clearly.
* If you correct something, make sure this does not then have a knock-on effect elsewhere in the text.

If you are proofreading professionally or marking proofs for printers, you should use standard proofreading marks. You can obtain these from any printing company.

Practice exercise

Proofread the following passage and correct any errors and inconsistencies. Check on page 195 to see how many you found.

> Bored staff can indeed spell danger for client's reputations. The key to avoiding this is to insure that the contact centre operators have knowlege and enthusiasm for the brand and are able to communicate that over the telephone. This is being succesfully achieved for Motorall by customer contact outsourcing partner Cloud Systems.
>
> Motorall are a passionate, visionery organisation who place considerable emphasise on committment

to the existing customer base. As part of this focus, a department was set up to deal with customers, with responsibility for reforming the Company to make it more customer driven and for building strong customer relationship.

A central element of this customer-conscious approach is an outsourced customer contact centre – the MOtorall Contact Centre (M.C.C.) – with the soul aim of talking to customers' correctly. By outsourcing, Motorall have a flexible resource to meet changing customer requirements. By insuring it choose the right partner, it sought to be "confident that the Motorall philosophy is fully understood and implemented'.

The MCC handle between 700 and 1,100 calls per week, generally 75% on cars, with the remaining ones evenly split between bikes and power products. The frequency of calls is heavily influenced by events (like motor shows, new model launches) and seasonality, which effects motorcycle and power equipment users. Additionally, MCC answers an average of two hundred and fifty emails and coupons per week on a wide range of topics.

Checklist

- Proofreading is the last task before handing over or sending a document.
- Leave a gap between writing and proofreading so you come to the task fresh.
- Familiarize yourself with your organization's house style.
- Read slowly and actively look for things that you know can go wrong.

Suggested style rules

If your organization has its own house style, you should follow that. However, here are some suggestions for a suitable style to use in business English.

Abbreviations

Use a final full stop after abbreviations only when the abbreviation would be confusing if the stop is omitted. (For example, write *no.* for 'number' to avoid confusion with the word 'no'). Otherwise don't use a full stop.

Avoid abbreviations within running text except with universally accepted names (*BBC*, *ITV*, *IBM*) and very common abbreviations (*eg*, *ie*, *etc*). Here is a list of common abbreviations which are likely to be used in business English:

am	before noon
C	Celsius (Centigrade)
c	century
c.	circa
cm	centimetre(s)
cwt	hundredweight(s)
eg	for example
etc	and so on
F	Fahrenheit
fl oz	fluid ounce(s)
ft	foot/feet
g	gram(s)
ie	that is

SUGGESTED STYLE RULES

→ in	inch(es)
K	Kelvin
kg	kilogram(s)
kJ	kilojoule(s)
km	kilometre(s)
kph/mph	kilometres per hour/ miles per hour
l	litre(s)
lb	pound(s)
m	metre(s)
ml	millilitre(s)
mm	millimetre(s)
NB	note well
oz	ounce(s)
pm	afternoon
UK	United Kingdom
US	United States
USA	United States of America
yd	yard(s)

Accents

Use accents on foreign words in common use in English only when they are vital for the pronunciation. This is particularly important if the word is a homonym of another (it is spelt the same as another word) but has a different meaning without the accent.

These common words should be written with accents:

> appliqué
>
> attaché
>
> bric-à-brac

canapé

café

cliché

crèche

déjà vu

exposé

façade

fête

naïve

pièce de résistance

précis

première

résumé

rosé

vis-à-vis

Capital letters

Capital letters should be used for people's names; the names of places, times, events, and institutions; and the titles of books, films, etc.

Use capitals for a job title only if it is used as part of the name; do not use capitals if the title is part of running text:

> *Steve Jones, Managing Director.*

> *The managing director, Steve Jones, said:*

Use capitals if the department name is part of a title; do not use capitals in running text:

Sarah Smith, Head of Marketing.

Sarah Smith works in the marketing department.

For headings and titles, use capitals for the first word only as well as for any names:

Re: Your order for 30 shirts.

Subject: Our meeting on 29 July.

Investigation report into health and safety hazards at the Bournemouth site.

Words such as *director, company, group, team* should be in lower case unless part of a title:

HMV Group plc

The company's profits grew

Use a capital for compass points when they are proper nouns; do not use a capital when they are used to describe location or direction:

The company is in the East Midlands.

Croydon is south of London.

Collective nouns

These nouns are always singular:

company

organization

enterprise

venture

government

school

partnership

They should therefore always be followed by the singular form of the verb:

> *The company announced its annual results.*
>
> *Brown & Co has launched a new product.*
>
> *The organization is closed until further notice.*
>
> *The government is facing a crisis over tax.*
>
> *The school is now top of the league tables.*

Other collective nouns – such as *staff, team, management, class, committee, group, family* – may be treated as a single entity (which takes the singular) or a group of individuals (which takes the plural), depending on the context:

> *The staff went for its annual party.*
>
> *The staff are at loggerheads with each other.*
>
> *The management made its decision.*
>
> *The management chose their different teams.*
>
> *The committee was locked away for hours.*
>
> *The committee were all re-elected.*
>
> *The committee weren't all re-elected: some lost their seats.*

Once you have decided whether a collective noun is either singular or plural, you must treat it consistently:

> ✗ *The management made its decision and then took their time in announcing the result.*
>
> ✔ *The management made its decision and then took its time in announcing the result.*
>
> ✔ *The management made their decision and then took their time in announcing the result.*

SUGGESTED STYLE RULES

Dates

Write dates in the following style:

>*24 July 2007*

No punctuation is needed.

Decades

Write the names of decades in numerals, without an apostrophe before the *s*:

>*1990s*

E-expressions

Use a hyphen when spelling the word *e-mail* as you would for other e-words, such as *e-commerce* and *e-broadcast*.

Foreign words

Unless they are in very common usage, foreign words should be written in italics.

Use italics for these expressions:

>*bon mot*
>
>*coup d'état*
>
>*bête noire*
>
>*raison d'être*
>
>*coup de grace*

Do not use italics for these very common words:

>entrepreneur
>
>cul-de-sac
>
>cliché
>
>à la carte

façade

élite

en suite

en route

Italics

Use italics for the following:

* titles of books, except for individual books of the Bible
* titles of periodicals
* titles of plays, films, radio and television programmes, operas, ballets, song cycles, etc
* titles of paintings and sculptures
* titles of record albums or collections of recorded works
* names of ships (but the letters HMS, SS, etc remain roman)
* foreign words which are not in common usage
* Latin names of biological genera, species and varieties
* names of parties in legal cases (but the letter 'v' between them remains roman)
* directions to the reader (eg *see also* or *above*)
* words given special emphasis

Numbers

All numbers up to and including nine should be spelt out as words; all numbers from 10 onwards should be as figures.

The exception is when a number is at the beginning of a sentence: the number should then be written as a word:

> *Eighty-eight people attended the meeting.*

SUGGESTED STYLE RULES

Use words for fractions. Fractions should be hyphenated:

> *three-quarters of the population*

> *two-thirds full*

Use figures in tables.

Percentages

Use *per cent* – written as two words – rather than the symbol % after all numbers, even if they are written as figures.

Phone numbers

When writing for a UK audience only, present telephone numbers with a space between the area code and the local number:

> *01223 123456*

When writing for an international audience, include an international code and put the opening zero in brackets:

> *+44 (0)1223 123456*

Sexism

Don't make assumptions that will alienate and annoy.

Avoid using *him* or *her* unless referring to a specific person:

> ✗ *Each telephonist will have a script on his screen.*

> ✗ *Each doctor will ensure she sees three patients in an hour.*

The best solution is to turn the sentence into the plural:

> *All telephonists will have a script on their screens.*

> *All doctors will ensure they see three patients an hour.*

Use the following occupation titles for both sexes:

author

firefighter

flight attendant

manager

mayor

poet

police officer

steward

usher

It is still acceptable to distinguish between sexes in the following cases:

actor/actress

chairwoman/chairman (if context does not allow *chair*)

spokeswoman/spokesman (but generally prefer *spokesperson*)

Solutions

Solutions

What is a sentence?
1 Complete sentence.
2 Fragment.
3 Fragment.
4 Complete sentence.
5 Complete sentence.
6 Fragment.

Keeping sentences short
1 *We seek to grow our business by offering innovative leathers. These will be differentiated from competing products by their performance properties, quality and consistency. They will also be backed by the highest standards of customer service.*

2 *Smith's share price is down and sales are under pressure. In addition, it has withdrawn some of its promotional activities. Now, the Health Protection Agency has linked the company to an outbreak of a rare strain of salmonella among 45 people by describing it as 'an exact match of that [strain] found in the product'.*

Joining sentences together
1 *It was a bright evening and the birds chirped in the trees.*
2 *It was a bright evening, the birds chirped in the trees, and Annie sat in the garden.*
3 *It was a bright evening but the house was dark when they arrived, so they turned on the lights.*
4 *We need to develop a new programme which will attract new customers, but we need to assure existing clients that this will not affect them.*
5 *We need to develop a new programme which will attract new*

customers, but we need to assure existing clients that this will not affect them, and we need to prove this to them.

Active and passive sentences

1   *Please organize your ideas and present them concisely.*
2   *I have examined the evidence and there seem to be grounds for disciplinary action. I have informed the managing director by letter and I expect his reply on Thursday.*
3   *During the programme, we will make outbound calls to customers to assess their willingness to purchase.*
4   *We will collect data and present this each month.*

Paragraphs

For a consulting company dedicated to improving healthcare through quality and business analysis, it was critical to find a flexible, reliable and low-cost solution that could grow with their needs. As a result of the Instorage architecture, which uses standard Ethernet switching for host and storage array connectivity, DHS achieves much better performance than its previous DAS environment.

The scalable Instorage solution enables DHS to expand the IP SAN using in-house resources. As a result, researchers have faster and more reliable access to data, enabling them to process and analyze patient records and test results more effectively. In addition, the company can start more research projects without concerns about storage capacity.

The best word for the job

1   *I called you about the folder I bought from you, and which I need to give to my committee tomorrow.*
2   *It would be useful for us to finish the project: we can change it at a date to be decided later.*
3   *They sent the invoice by fax, with extra information, but it was clear they hadn't made the changes.*
4   *It would be helpful to us if you could carry out the repairs by using the latest parts.*

5 *The holidays affected our plans but this showed we need more staff.*

Tautology, pleonasm and redundancy
1 *Entrance is for ticket-holders only: the reason is lack of planning caused by the crisis.*
2 *In the past, innovations have been essential.*
3 *There is no alternative. The consensus is that prospects will divide the nation.*
4 *The gift was a bonus; we offered our thanks.*
5 *It was unanimous: the plate was perfect.*

Put the action into the verb
1 *We know he will deliver the package on Tuesday.*
2 *When we met him, he proposed changing the name.*
3 *From today, all ideas should be submitted to the management team.*
4 *The team then discussed seating.*
5 *Callit launched the product in Amsterdam.*

Apostrophes
1 *Its mother decided it was time to give its child its milk.*
2 *The lady gave some eggs and tomatoes to her children's friends.*
3 *During the 1980s, the government's policy was to reduce its spending.*
4 *In two years' time, it will have completed its term as a blind person's companion.*
5 *It's time to decide whose friend you are and who's going to go with you.*
6 *The book was theirs; it wasn't hers.*
7 *There was a month's gap between its first and last win.*

Commas
1 *The carpet, which is soiled, is going to be replaced.*
2 *Although they wanted to go, they stayed inside.*
3 *He implied that some, if not all, of the proposal was wrong.*

4   *We have sent the goods, although they may take time to reach you.*
5   *They held a discussion, and afterwards they had a meal together.*

Colons

1   *Chris Beattie, who made the device, believes it will fill a gap in the market: 'Our research shows there is considerable demand.'*
2   *The interviews were held in various rooms: offices, hallways, the reception area.*
3   *David couldn't leave the office on time: he needed to finish his report.*
4   *The team were devastated: no orders and no prospect of any for at least a month.*

Semicolons

1   *Peter wanted to pay the full amount; John did not. An argument ensued.*
2   *The course comprised a number of units: elementary English, including punctuation; clear writing, with lots of exercises; and practical exercises.*
3   *The screen is bright and clear; the keyboard is small and compact.*

Brackets

1   *The shop (Choc a Lot) was closed on Fridays.*
2   *We looked at it [the estate] and decided to buy.*
3   *The loaf (loaves) must then be left in the oven for 10 minutes.*
4   *The gallery contained the finest examples of Impressionist art (Monet, Gauguin, Degas).*

Dashes

1   *He knew he had won – but not by that much.*
2   *The team knew the prospective customer – a tough operator – would be difficult to win over.*
3   *She had seen him before and talked to him – without permission.*
4   *They collected the materials – wire, connectors, plugs and brackets – and started to put them together.*

Common mistakes

1 How does this _affect_ you?

2 There were _adverse_ trading conditions which _affected_ our profit.

3 He _alluded_ to her in his speech but I can _assure_ you it was accidental.

4 The manager was responsible for _appraising_ the team based on the number of successful sales calls each month.

5 He set a trap with the wallet as _bait_ and watched with _bated_ breath.

6 It was not a pretty _sight_: compared _with_ the last visit, it had changed out of all recognition.

7 He _complimented_ me on my delivery style, but I wasn't _complacent_: he would expect more next time.

8 She talked _continuously_, which meant we couldn't hear the performance.

9 We've been asked to _copywrite_ the leaflet: it needs to _complement_ the website.

10 His _counsel_ was different _from_ the previous advice we had received.

11 The building was _destroyed_ by the fire.

12 There were three _criteria_: weight, size and height.

13 She went to the meeting, _despite_ her misgivings.

14 She is so _efficient_: everything is always delivered on time.

15 He was _disinterested_ and made the perfect referee.

16 The report _elicited_ a swift response.

17 The desk was _discrete_ from the table – at least four _metres_ away.

18 They _defused_ the situation by announcing it was time for lunch.

19 The decision was _imminent_: then we would be entering the next _phase_.

20 They refused to listen to any _further_ demands.

21 We had no cause to worry: the material was _non-flammable_.

22 They summarized the report verbally for the marketing director and _me_.

23 He _flaunted_ his credentials but he wasn't offered the job.

24 I was late so I had to _forgo_ the first session.

25 There was a secret _hoard_ of stationery in the cabinet.

SOLUTIONS

26 The factory needed _less_ wool than before and produced _fewer_ jumpers.

27 The garage was _licensed_ by the DVLA.

28 We had _led_ the market but we could _lose_ our position unless we increase productivity.

29 None of the interviewees _was_ suitable for the job.

30 The new production line will _mitigate_ the impact of shorter working hours.

31 We needed to be _practical_: it just wasn't _practicable_ to get there and back in two hours.

32 They were _past_ caring.

33 The council _meted_ out fines to all transgressors.

34 It was common _practice_ to leave early on a Friday.

35 We could see he was _prevaricating_ because he simply wasn't ready.

36 We followed all the _principles_ we had been taught by our parents.

37 The client told us to end the contract, _which_ was a bit of a blow.

38 When I arrive, _whom_ should I contact?

39 I had run out of _stationery_, so I rang the supplier.

40 The money we'd set aside for tax was _sequestrated_ by the officials.

Quiz

1 They felt that they had one, and only one, chance to succeed.

2 The company was astonished at the quality but still stuck to its decision.

3 In 12 years' time they will reach their maximum.

4 There are a number of items you will need to bring: paper with complementary envelopes; pens, preferably red, black and blue; CDs; staplers, and paper clips.

5 It's time to decide whether you are going to add to the team.

6 She handed it to Gavin and me: the effect was immediate.

7 She was so impressed with my writing that she compared it to Shakespeare's!

8 Only ten people applied for the job, which was far fewer than she expected.

9 The pharmacy lost its licence: the reason was lack of organization.

10 Annie forgot her PIN when she went to the ATM.

11 *The government's new policy had further impact on the price of PCs.*

12 *In the 1990s, the company's managing director was appointed for three years' service.*

13 *There were only two words for it: really terrible!*

14 *While he was out of the room, the team enquired about the prospects for the organization.*

15 *The consensus was that the brochure was perfect, but it would have to be replaced in six months' time.*

16 *The children's teacher would not divulge anything on principle.*

17 *Trefoil was determined not to lose the contract, but it was faced with a bleak outlook.*

18 *In the morning, as soon as I'm awake, I put my phone on: it's part of the job.*

19 *None of the team wants to go, although it would have been fun.*

20 *Sayed was satisfied: the delegates had listened, learnt and worked hard; now they were really going to think about their use of the English language.*

SOLUTIONS

Letters

Here is an improved version of the letter on page 89:

The IT Centre
50 Oxford Street
Bournemouth
BH1 9AA

19 November 2007

Mr P Smith
1 The Avenue
New Malden
Surrey
KT3 1BB

Dear Mr Smith

Following our telephone conversation earlier today, I enclose the 30 ink cartridges you requested.

As discussed, we do not have any more of these in stock at the moment but we believe we will receive further stocks soon. I will contact you as soon as I have any more news about this.

I would be very grateful if you could let me know that you have received this order. In the meantime, many thanks for your business.

Yours sincerely

Paul Jones
Warehouse Manager

E-mails

Here is an improved version of the e-mail on page 97:

To: Barbara@bathson.co.uk
From: Nigel.marr@brightlights.com
Re: Lighting Order 7th November 2007

Dear Ms Bathson

Many thanks for your order dated 7th November for seven Macintosh glass lampholders and three pull switches. We're pleased to inform you that we have a special offer at the moment, which will mean you will receive the seven lampholders for the price of six.

We expect to despatch these items to you tomorrow (9th November) for delivery the following day but will let you know if this changes.

Many thanks once again for your custom.

Kind regards.

Nigel Marr

Nigel Marr
Senior Sales Consultant
Bright Lights Ltd
1 The Promenade, Weston super Mare BS22 1AB
01934 654321
www.brightlights.com

SOLUTIONS

Reports

Here is an improved version of the report on pages 117–18:

ASTEROID ELECTRO MECHANICAL SYSTEMS PLC

Investigation report into health and safety hazards at the Bournemouth site

Date of submission: 25 June 2007
Compiled by: PD Smith, Safety Officer
For the attention of: GH Merryweather, Managing Director

1. Terms of Reference
This report is the result of an investigation into health and safety hazards at the Bournemouth site which may contravene the Health and Safety at Work Act.

It was requested by the Managing Director to prepare for the visit by the Government Inspector which may take place at an unspecified date. It was carried out by the newly appointed Safety Officer and was to be submitted by the end of June 2007. The report should recommend any possible health and safety improvements.

2. Methods of Investigation

2.1. Legislation: The Health & Safety at Work Act was studied.

2.2. Observation: The Research and Development Annex, the Production Workshops and the office-based departments (Personnel, Finance and Marketing) were inspected. Two hours were spent in each location, observing and taking notes.

2.3. Interviews: The line managers for each location were interviewed to find out if they had seen any problems. They were also asked how well they knew their own responsibilities under the Act.

2.4. Informal discussions: These were carried out with some employees during the observations.

3. Findings/analysis of information

3.1. Legislation: The legislation makes it clear that all staff could be liable under the Act if an accident occurs. It clarifies responsibilities for senior management, supervisory staff and all other employees. A short guide can be found in Appendix 1.

3.2. Observation:

3.2.1. R&D Annex: This is a 'clean' environment and conditions are generally good. However, one graduate trainee was observed attempting to lift a heavy CO_2 cylinder. When questioned, he stated

---

he had been asked to do this by the project leader and that all personnel had to do this to ensure tests could continue.

3.2.2. The workshops: There seemed to be no problems in most workshops. In Workshop C, however, the ventilation had broken down and as it was a very hot day staff were working with open coats. There was a danger of these catching in the machinery.

3.2.3. The offices: Generally, these had good working conditions. However, there were too many extension leads in the administration office and these were trailing across the floor. There appeared to be a general carelessness over trailing leads in all offices.

3.2.4. Interviews:

a) The Project Manager: when asked about the CO_2 cylinders, the project manager stated that he had lifted them on occasions. One trainee had suffered from a strained back. Trolleys had been requested from the R&D Manager but none had been delivered.

b) The Workshop C Supervisor: when asked about the ventilation, the workshop supervisor stated that a request for action had been made to Maintenance in writing a week earlier but the reply indicated that Maintenance was short-staffed because of holidays but would respond as soon as possible. The workshop supervisor understood his responsibilities, which had been covered in a training course.

c) Two relevant office supervisors: both indicated that extension leads were needed.

3.2.5. Informal discussions with employees: there was a lack of awareness over possible liability under the Act. All employees however had signed contracts of employment which stated that they were responsible for their own safety.

4. Conclusions

4.1. There is no suitable lifting method for the CO_2 cylinders. The company would be liable if this caused a back injury.

4.2. There are not sufficient staff in the maintenance department to repair the ventilation.

4.3. There is considerable danger from trailing leads in many departments.

4.4. Staff in many departments are unsure about safety procedures.

5. Recommendations

5.1. Industrial Lifting Gear plc should be contacted immediately to solve the lack of lifting equipment.

5.2. Four extra temporary maintenance staff should be employed. Both the ventilation in workshop C and the number of power sockets in the Administration Office should be addressed as a matter of priority.

5.3. There should be safety courses organized for all staff, run by the Training Office. Safety should also form an important part of induction days for all new staff.

SOLUTIONS

Preparing an electronic presentation
1 Here is an improved version of the top slide on page 128:

How to proceed: 10 Top Tips

⌘ Get support   ⌘ Be first in your sector
⌘ Go global   ⌘ Don't wait to be perfect
⌘ Map the benefits v brand value   ⌘ Allow time after launch
⌘ Set clear objectives   ⌘ Guidelines visibly in place
⌘ Business before technology   ⌘ Experiment

---

2 Here is an improved version of the bottom slide on page 128:

Managing Complex Change

You need:

Vision + skills + incentive + resources + action plan

⌘ No vision = confusion
⌘ No skills = anxiety
⌘ No action plan = false starts
⌘ No resources = frustration
⌘ No incentive = gradual change

Summarizing

Here is a 67-word summary of the report on pages 117–18:

> *This report is the result of an investigation into health and safety hazards at the Bournemouth site. It has been produced using both desk and field research. Its findings are that there are specific areas which need attention, in particular the lifting of CO_2 cylinders, ventilation in workshops, trailing leads and staff knowledge. It makes a number of recommendations which will provide both immediate and long-term solutions.*

Proofreading

Here is a corrected version of the passage on pages 169–70. Corrections appear in bold type. This version assumes the use of the house style suggested on pages 171–9.

> *Bored staff can indeed spell danger for **clients'** reputations. The key to avoiding this is to **ensure** that the contact centre operators have **knowledge** and enthusiasm for the brand and are able to communicate that over the telephone. This is being **successfully** achieved for Motorall by customer contact outsourcing partner Cloud Systems.*
>
> *Motorall is a passionate, **visionary organization** **which places** considerable **emphasis** on **commitment** to the existing customer base. As part of this focus, a department was set up to deal with customers, with responsibility for reforming the **company** to make it more customer driven and for building strong customer **relationships**.*
>
> *A central element of this customer-conscious approach is an outsourced customer contact centre – the **Motorall** Contact Centre (**MCC**) – with the **sole** aim of talking to **customers** correctly. By*

outsourcing, Motorall **has** a flexible resource to meet changing customer requirements. By **ensuring** it **chose** the right partner, it sought to be 'confident that the Motorall philosophy is fully understood and implemented'.

The MCC **handles** between 700 and 1,100 calls per week, generally split **75 per cent** on cars, with the remaining ones evenly split between bikes and power products. The frequency of calls is heavily influenced by events (like motor shows, new model launches) and seasonality, which **affects** motorcycle and power equipment users. Additionally, **the** MCC answers an average of **250 e-mails** and coupons per week on a wide range of topics.

Index

INDEX

INDEX